# THE

# RESURRECTION

## OF HUMANITY

# THE
# RESURRECTION
## OF HUMANITY

BY OM

ISBN: 978-1-4269-5774-1 (sc)
ISBN: 978-1-4269-5775-8 (e)

*Trafford rev. 03/01/2011*

 www.trafford.com

North America & international
toll-free: 1 888 232 4444 (USA & Canada)
phone: 250 383 6864 ◆ fax: 812 355 4082

# THE RESURRECTION OF I IUMANITY

## by Om

This book is unlike any other because it offers not only the truth of our existence and purpose in life, which thousands of others have, but also the only plan of action that can save us from total destruction and the extinction of humanity, which is occurring regardless of what people believe, because of our decreasing levels of consciousness. The extinction of humanity will not come from physical destruction, it will come from memory loss of true self. We are literally on the verge of forgetting ourselves. Our lines of consciousness are so out of alignment that we can barely remember what we do day to day. Our brains are capable of photographic memory and instant recall of all stored memory but we've forgotten how to access it. Forgetfulness, Alzheimer's, amnesia, and cancer are at epidemic levels. Cancer is also memory loss, just at the cellular level. Every disorder and aging is a result of separation from Self, causing memory loss. Even the Cosmos shows these horrifying disorganized patterns of energy. There's not one visualization of supernovas or galaxies being perfectly spherical, having perfectly concentric circles, or linear lines of energy in the arms of galaxies. Supernovas should create perfect circles of colour as they expand out and all the particles of matter spiraling around a center point making galaxies, should be in perfectly spiraling lines as they are being pulled and pushed, creating perfectly geometrical patterns, but instead the colours are mixed through and the lines are jagged and missing. The only perfectly geometrical patterns being created are crop circles and nature which are made by the magnetic energy of Mother Earth's love.

This book of divine inspiration, is a gift, a message, and a blessing, but also a cry for help and a warning. It is being sent by the unconsciousness of every living entity, through our subconscious mind that has been plagued with generations of denial and memory loss, to our conscious mind. People all over the world are feeling an uneasiness, like a gut feeling, which is our inner self trying to tell us that there is a purpose in life that we have not yet accomplished, and we are running out of time. People all over the world are also feeling the need to find spiritual enlightenment, and have at least once in their life, felt a connection to their higher inner self, which is often experienced as a premonition, deja vu, vision, dream or enlightenment. Unfortunately, when people experience this truly divine connection, they frequently perceive it as a force outside of themselves like God, Allah, guardian angels and others. The moment they think that it is not their own force or center being, they return to the reality they've been taught to believe in.

They fail to understand it's meaning, so they ignore the message and eventually forget about it, or they put all their faith into a religion that supports the idea that the power of the experience came from a force greater than their own. The truth is, we are the power. Our Self is the Creator of our own reality. Any separate consciousness, like God, Brahma, or Allah, would have their own perception, their own illusion of life, unless of course you are the consciousness of God, Brahma, or Allah, in which case you are God, Brahma, and Allah, and is the only thing that makes sense. This is the message being sent to all of us. We are the consciousness of the Whole, and the creator of our own reality. We share our reality with others by accepting theirs as part of our expansion creating a consensus reality. However, as long as we believe in this consensus reality of death and total destruction, we will manifest this horrifying extinction of humanity and Gaia.

If the destruction of humanity and Gaia, our Earth mother, does occur, there would be no one to blame except ourselves because the original descent of humanity was a horrible, but unintentional mistake. If we choose not to accept the knowledge being given to us, and ignore our responsibility to bring salvation to humanity and the Cosmos through unity, we, the descendants of humanity, who have been given Divine intervention to be here at this particular time, and are the only ones with the power to correct this horrible descent, will have deliberately brought an end to our existence. A nuclear annihilation will prevent Gaia from ascension, causing her and all life in, on and around her to fragment, and if she does ascend, the cells of every life form that is not resonating at a high enough level will spontaneously combust, creating fire and destruction all around the globe, known as Hell, as predicted in the Bible and many other books that predict the future. The Bible predicts this time of horrifying destruction to also be the resurrection of some. However, the resurrection is not of those who believe that the power is from Christ, but those who believe that the power is from within themselves. Only you can increase your vibration to a higher level. Others like Christ, can only remind us that we are alive, and show us ways to increase our levels of consciousness. Fragmenting is when your thoughts of being become separated and lost from each other, bringing total darkness to your mind. Without the memory of thought, you're unable to create a synergistic thought, allowing for the process of forming an idea. If you can't create ideas, you'll never form any intentions, including the intention to sustain your own physical life, like Alzheimer's. If people with Alzheimer's didn't have others providing the essentials of life to them, they would die, and when they passed on, they would have no memories to remind them of who they are, causing their consciousness to become completely fragmented. Alzheimer's and cancer are the most feared of all diseases, because cancer is memory loss at the cellular level, and Alzheimer's is memory loss of the mind!! Remember, the physical destruction of our physical world is not what we should fear the most, it is the massive memory loss of humanity, known as extinction. If by the time of transformation, December 2012, we don't have the awareness of our true inner self, we will become fragmented, because only through our love for ourselves, will we be able to hold our thoughts and memories together. Becoming lost from yourself is referred to as being "removed from the Book of Life", because life is creation, the expansion of self, and if you lose the memory of self, you lose the ability to create, to live. Once you're fragmented, you will remain in total darkness until someone else touches you and gives you enough loving energy to remind you that you are alive, but have become lost, and only by returning to your inner self, will you ever become your true self. The only way to return to your inner self is by having a perfectly healthy body and mind, and remembering your life through focused thought.

Unfortunately, the governments around the world are doing all they can to keep us from finding ourselves. As long as they keep people in a state of fear, like losing their job and not being able to pay their bills or get food, contracting a deadly disease, being tortured by a criminal, losing their loved ones, or worse of all, developing Alzheimer's, they can continue to control them. Their only purpose is to dominate us by keeping us separated from our inner soul, our Self. All the toxins in our foods, water and air, and mental anguish of being poor, sick, or ridiculed for expressing ourselves, are preventing us from connecting to our higher inner self. Even people who are currently reviving their physical body to crystalline patterns of energy and increasing their level of consciousness, giving them the ability to teach us how to, are frequently pulled into darkness because of the severity of evil that is governing our world. By bringing perfect health and vitality to our bodies, we'll feel the joy and happiness that will allow us to love each other, and respect all our differences, giving us resurrection, not destruction. We have all become bound to each other in this physical system, referred to as the Cosmos, and are dependent on each other's love to reunite us so that we may evolve to the next level of life.

This book was written purely as a gift to all of humanity, nature, and the Cosmos. The information contained within is the truth about all life, past, present, and future, how evil was created and obtained dominion over humanity, and most importantly, how every single person and life form can be cured of all ailments, including aging, and together can save our world from destruction. We have all been chosen to be alive on Gaia at this time because we have the love, courage and understanding, to make the greatest changes in all of human history. To rejoin together in love and harmony, and regain our ability to manifest our own realities, and not be trapped in others. Each and every one of us has evolved from the thought of not being nothingness, through the creation of definition, and expanded that definition into a physical universe, and bodily form, that we are now part of. As long as we are bound to our physical world, we must understand the laws of physical manifestation. We are the genetic continuation of our parents and ancestors, but we have the gift to transcend that form into a pure crystalline form by finding all karmic attachments held in our DNA that are distorting our form, release them through love and forgiveness, and resurrect our bodies as Christ did, bringing salvation to all our ancestors and all other species.

Through teachings of Frank Hatem, Dr. Pier Luigi Ighina, and Karen Danrich, I've come to understand that magnetic energy is the constant and infinite movement between thought and love that creates and moves energy, which condenses and forms matter, and then organizes matter into compounds and biological life. All life began when we became aware that we were not nothingness. We became aware of this because we could feel our self. The self is the embodiment of nothingness. It encompasses the nothingness, making nothingness the centre, the periphery infinity, and the embodiment our universe. To expand the embodiment through creation is known as living and is our infinite goal. However, there is a constant desire to unite as ONE, meaning all the movements of energy would become completely synchronous, but to become ONE would mean losing all identity of the Self. Without definition of Self there is only ONE, a nothingness yet everything, the alpha and the omega, life and the absence of life, the light and the dark, the yin and the yang, the father and the mother. This is the duality of our existence. Not being nothingness and nothingness. Being one and being the whole. Creation and the unity of creation. Separation and togetherness. Out of the necessity to be something, the Self must reject total unity by expanding further, creating more life. Magnetic energy is this perpetual movement of attraction, love, and repulsion, creation. That's all life is. Creating and loving what you create! There are beautiful people all over the world that are extremely intelligent, insightful, and evolved who are ascending their forms and know the true history of humanity. They can help us all to achieve the greatness that they are achieving, and stop the destruction of our world. Everyone knows what the future will be if we don't stop this destruction right now, which is why we must stop the injustices and pollution that is destroying our world, and choose these amazing people as our leaders before we descend into total chaos and darkness.

This in no way implies that I, the author of this book, have reached this higher level of consciousness, nor have I heard this information from the "voice of God". I simply had a spiritual encounter, as millions have, and touched this universal truth which the Divine is desperately trying to get to all of us. For years I've tried to convince myself that since I had no position of political, spiritual, financial or intellectual authority, and no means of getting the people to listen to me, that I was not worthy to make such a statement. I kept waiting for someone else like a top political figure, holy person, or renowned scientist to come forward with this truly divine knowledge, but they haven't. The truth is being revealed to us all over the world through these people who are at higher levels of consciousness, but only to those looking for it. Unfortunately, most of the people don't look for it. They look to news and the history and discovery channels for truth, and to their church for spiritual guidance. They're actually criticized for not believing in these systems, so they look no further.

Scientists and scholars have put so much time and effort in trying to discover the truth of our creation, and the mechanics of the universe, that they resist accepting the simple solutions to these questions. However, now that truth has been revealed, it's time we admit that the truth has been misrepresented in religions and ancient archives, and demand to know the truth, and change our world into one that will not only save us from total extinction, but bring perfect health back to our bodies and minds, allowing us to ascend to higher levels like archangels and Christ. This is what Christ truly tried to teach us and help us to understand and believe in. If humanity would start raising their level of consciousness by looking up keywords on the internet like ascension, mental powers, chakras, alchemy of time, sacred geometry, magnetic atom, and crop circles, they would start understanding all the information that has been hidden from us by our ancestors who feared losing their false sense of dominion.

People have been taught since the time of their birth, especially those who are descendants of institutions that govern our world, that the truth must remain hidden at all costs, that their financial and political status makes them superior to others, and that dominion over humanity is the only purpose in life worth having. It is this belief that creates the darkness that is consuming our lives, and it is those who are so driven by this darkness, that must save us. The true saviors of humanity won't be Christ or Allah, it will be the criminals, the bankers and the politicians. I wanted to believe that no one could possibly hold the knowledge that would save all of humanity, that there is no chosen one, but I'm constantly being faced with messages from movies, video games and books showing me otherwise. We are all chosen ones with a specific purpose, and mine must be to finish this book and get it released to the world, because I've reached a point where my every waking moment is thinking about this responsibility, and feeling a stronger sense of panic that I'm running out of time! I realize that if I don't accomplish this purpose in giving everyone this information that I've been given, that I have failed, and am continuing to bring more death to the Divine, because the more we die, the Whole dies. This is not new information, because as I said, it's being revealed all over the world, but it is a plan that can bring love and life to all people of this world. I have no wishes to receive money for this book, because it doesn't belong to me, but to the world. However, I do need you to help me get it out there. I also have no wishes to become a leader, but I will do whatever I need to do to help save humanity from total destruction, which I've come to believe will occur in a couple of years if we don't do something about it right now.

The Mayan Calendar, the I Ching, the Hopi Indians, Revelations and scientists have all predicted this. Some say that it is just going to be a transformation, like it has happened before, but this knowledge that I received spiritually, tells me that this is Gaia's twelfth, and last chance for ascension and if she tries to ascend without the ascension of humanity, she will fragment, as humanity is part of her whole. Gaia holds the memory of us all through her love, and she is sending her love to each and every one of us in attempts to help us remember who we are. That's why Christ was always portrayed as praying in the wilderness alone. Gaia knows the pathways, also known as Taos, that will show us our way back to our soul. When our physical bodies die, it is only our thoughts and emotions that will live on, that is as long as we can remember them. Life is mind and when we forget how to create loving and creative thoughts, we stop living. We are cancer to the Divine because we have forgotten our spiritual essence and purpose in life, and without that awareness there is no unity, no light, and we all die. The Divine dies! We are the consciousness of the Divine and if we fail to wake up from this horrible pit of forgetfulness that we have been trapped in for trillions of generations, we will sink into total darkness for eternity. This darkness steals our memories, and without memory of an original creative thought we can't remember who we are, and will simply exist in the illusion of how others see us. However, if the illusion of others is total darkness, then so will be ours. We, the descendants, who are the consciousness of the Divine, determine whether the Divine, which is the Whole of us, lives or dies. The only way the Divine can live is by us healing our physical, mental and spiritual bodies, and finding our own unique path that leads us to the next level of evolution. This is our time for resurrection!

This incredible book offers truth that can preserve our existence, and solve the questions to all mysteries, and challenges any top scientist, scholar or spiritual leader, to present evidence against it. This knowledge can reveal the answers to questions like, who are we? Where did we come from? How was our universe and the entire cosmos created? Are the life forms referred to as extraterrestrial beings distant family members? Are movies like Powder, Contact, and Star Trek, actually a reality in the history of humanity? Is telepathy, telekinesis and teleportation a natural part of life? Are crop circles energy patterns that evoke higher levels of consciousness? Is it possible to give every single person on Gaia their dream life, completely free of depression, disease and disorder, and full of fun, love and peace? Societies worldwide spend enormous amounts of money and time trying to find the truth to these questions but still cannot even understand how, why, and by whom were megalithic structures constructed, how ancient civilizations have predicted our future, and how we are connected to the universe? We can't answer these questions because we have forgotten. The truth is that everyone of us are perfect energy forms, created from the magnificent thought of being alive.

The scientific world demands physical proof, but rejects the true movement of life, magnetic energy. Humanity has forgotten the true past which is why we can't figure out ancient creations, and continue to repeat history over and over again, also known as a "loop of time". This explains how our future can be predicted, because it is actually our past that is being repeated, and will continue unless there is a total fragmentation of all humanity, or we wake up and realize who we really are, and find our place in the universe which will expand our mind and form to higher levels of consciousness. There are two types of dimensions; higher levels of consciousness and previous lives that are being repeated. Higher levels of consciousness are experienced as a magical and spiritual connection to the universe, whereas previous lives are memories, like deja vues, and premonitions, that remind us that we are continuing our same past life, keeping us concentrated and stuck at our current level of consciousness. We have learned to live in the past, pray for the future, and ignore the present. These destructive thoughts have been passed down through generation after generation because they are encoded into our DNA, and will continue to replicate until people become aware of these negative thoughts that are distorting our DNA and level of consciousness, and release their karmic attachments through love and forgiveness, which will allow us to ascend past this point of distortion. The cellular structure of a fully conscious person holds thousands of strands of DNA and utilize 100% of their brain capacity, whereas the average person holds only 2 strands of DNA and utilize less than 10% of their brain capacity. Imagine what you could do if you used 100% of your brain capacity, with all your cells and chakras moving in harmony with each other. This is our birth right, and can be our reality if we join together and restore true health to Gaia and ourselves. There has always been evidence encrypted in languages and parables that explains this vast knowledge, but modern man has failed to decipher them until now. There has been physical evidence of true history and the power of thoughts, which has been presented all over the world, but has failed to become public knowledge because the evil in the world wants to keep us in the dark and hidden from all knowledge of truth.

In 1955 Leon Raoul Hatem discovered that magnetism, which is simply love for self, creates and moves all energy with the infinite goal to always create more life and love all that is created. Our thought of being alive, known as the Self, is the feeling that we are separate of nothingness and of other life. We define ourselves through the duality of nothingness and of being. The duality attracts each other but when too close will fall upon each other, becoming one, so through necessity of being, repulse each other, pushing the thoughts out, creating more life. This constant attraction and repulsion creates the vibration of each entity, and the more creative the thoughts, the stronger the love, and the higher the vibration. Through Dr. Pier Luigi Ighina's, understanding of magnetism and vibration, he designed an apparatus that changed the molecular structure of a peach tree into an apple tree by changing the vibration of a peach tree to the vibration of an apple tree, and healed a deformed bone by raising the vibration to that of a healthy bone, within a few days. NASA experiments have proven that cells removed from someone's body and taken many miles away, still respond to the mental thoughts of that person. Dr. Masaru Emoto has proven that the power of thoughts and spoken words can change the structure of water molecules from a blob of dark and disorganized patterns to perfect crystalline and colorful patterns. Karen Danrich and Thomas Weber have proven that communication with all our ancestors and Gaia's kingdoms is possible and the process of spiritual ascension, including the reversal of disease and aging, can be a reality for everyone who believes and works hard to accomplish it. Dr. John Lerma has published stories revealing spiritual knowledge obtained during cancer patients pre-death experiences. Partial truth is found in bones, writings and artifacts and relies mainly on hypothesis and interpretation. Absolute truth is found telepathically which can only be done by connecting with your higher inner self and then connecting yourself with the higher energies of other life forms. This absolute truth can be everyone's reality if the people all over the world would take all the money being spent on wars and research, and misappropriated in accounts and organizations, and use it to create the true Garden of Eden. The true Garden of Eden has never existed before because it is a consciousness of new creative thought after experiencing a total lack of new thought. Since humanity is the life form that experienced this descent of consciousness and started living in the past, it's humanity who must reunite all life forms together and transform ourselves and Gaia, into the healthy and vibrant life forms that we once were and should be again, so we can gather all the life we created and internalize it into our being. Gaia and ascending people can show us how to cleanse our bodies and minds of all toxins and learn how to increase our levels of consciousness.

The Americans have been chosen to be the first to receive this incredible book because number one, I, the simple messenger of this Divine Plan, am an American, and number two, it is the Americans that are of all cultures who hold positions of authority in financial and political institutions, and because the Americans are most being manipulated by the mind controlling agents and toxins in our foods, water supplies and medicines. This book is a gift to the whole world containing the Divine truth about the creation of life, the creation of evil, and the only solution that will eliminate evil by bringing light back to all darkened areas. It is also a desperate cry for help from all our ancestors who realize that we are on the edge of extinction, and can only be saved by learning to love and respect each other's differences, and forgiving all our ancestors that passed their mistakes down to us, by eliminating all toxins from our bodies and minds and those in all kingdoms of nature, and joining as ONE, which is our true spiritual essence, the Whole. Everyone needs to admit the truth about what is happening in our world today. Nearly everyone is desperately focused on obtaining money because without it you can't afford to buy what you need in life to survive, are considered worthless by the multitudes if you don't have it, and now, again, will actually be imprisoned for not having it. The elite few from around the world, referred to as the secret society, are constantly changing our environment and lives, based on power and greed which has been instilled upon them since they were born. They govern the institutions and organizations that create these toxins and diseases, and design ways to keep people distracted from the truth, focused on worldly possessions, and addicted to toxins that are hidden in our air, foods, drinks and medications. They have put laws in effect that actually protect doctors who make lethal decisions, causing wrongful death and disfigurement to us and our loved ones, and laws that protect the financial status of wealthy organizations which has allowed our government to give them the hard earned money from the citizens taxes, which these organizations then blatantly spend in any reckless way they choose. They have such control over our lives that no one is safe. Even those who consider themselves as the wealthy are currently experiencing how the government can take their invested money, as they've done before, leaving them broke and in despair. No one is safe from this darkness unless we unite together!

People want to close their eyes to the truth because the truth is frightening. They would rather believe in a savior that will remove them from all harm and darkness. However, this secret society is the true saviors of all humanity, because it is those who are in the extreme boundaries of darkness and completely governed by evil that must find their way back to the light. These leaders that rule over our world will become the true leaders of humanity. Not Jesus, Mohammed, Buddha, Krishna and more, but them and all of us! It is up to us, the descendants of humanity, who must stop the evil that is devouring our total existence, and restore life to the Whole. Now is the time when all the loving energies of the Cosmos are being sent to Gaia that will help us remember what we've forgotten, because Gaia is the last living natal planet that holds the knowledge for our ascension. The Divine, which is the Whole of us all, has also chosen us because we believe that we have enough compassion, strength and determination to succeed. It would take an extremely strong person to stand up and admit that they've been wrong, and everything that has been taught to them is a misrepresentation of the truth. It would also be extremely difficult for a rich person to surrender their power by creating a non-monetary system and equal rights for all. The moment we all, including serial killers, military generals, and world bankers, remember the truly beautiful people we are, all of humanity can find their paths of alignment, allowing them to evolve to the next higher level. However, if the words in this book do not unite the leaders of our world and bring light into their hearts, it will be up to the people's strength and courage to stand against them, admit the truth about our creation and religions, and make the changes ourselves. People all over the world with financial, political, scientific and spiritual knowledge far greater than my own, are ready to use their gifts in bringing health and harmony to our world, they just need a plan that will protect them and give them all the resources they need to accomplish it.

This plan has been divinely sent and is known as the Holistic Governance! This book describes the steps in setting the foundations of this new world law, which is love, meaning that every law is based on an idea that encourages growth of consciousness, and the betterment of all people and life forms, the Whole, including life forms in other dimensions, galaxies, and universes. Some people believe that it will take hundreds and thousands of years to see this happen but in reality this can be done in one year because time is speeding up and what took thousands of years to accomplish is currently taking only a few years. If the financial and political controllers of our world joined together, they could immediately stop all wars, return everyone back to their homes, which is the place that resonates with them, reunite families and friends, evaluate everyone's weaknesses and strengths, and provide every single person with all the resources needed to live their true dream life. By stopping all the pollution and stripping of natural resources Gaia can change the water back to a pure crystalline structure that will nurture every cell in our bodies, and restore balance in the soils, minerals, plants and animals. With a balance in her energies there would be no natural disasters or famines, only an abundance of beauty and recreation, and all life forms would live in harmony. No more insect bites, or roaches in buildings. If we bring health back to our bodies and environment we'll have a mutual respect for all life, and all life will live in harmony with each other.

The truth is that we are all perfect images of the Divine, therefore we are all equally important. Everyone has the ability to find their inner force and turn their life into whatever they want, which is what has always been intended for us to do. We can reach levels of telepathy, telekinesis and teleportation simply by cleansing our bodies, souls and minds from all toxins and raising our level of self awareness. Every single person has the innate ability to communicate with their indigenous animal, plant, insect and mineral kingdoms, cure every ailment from mental retardation, mental illness, paralysis, cancer, heart disease and any other immune disease, and re-grow missing limbs, teeth, organs and glands. We all have stem cells that hold the memory of the pure spiritual essence of every single cell that was part of our original perfect body, and when commanded by the mind can regenerate any cell, correcting every deformity and reversing all aspects of aging. People's appearances of adult age, would return to their state of perfect physical maturation, which is typically twenties for women and thirties for men. The fountain of youth is truly mind over matter. People born with deformities and disorders, including disproportionate facial and body features would change their appearances into their true nature that would be considered as cute, beautiful, or handsome. Spontaneous regeneration is possible with a fully conscious mind.

There is proof that the DNA in every gene of every cell in our bodies, and the bodies of every single life form on and of Gaia, has been mutated by the radioactivity and carcinogens that are constantly influencing the movement of energy within our cells. When the energy is resonant, meaning that the vibration feels good to you, your cells will return to their original speed of movement. This allows them to spin in the right direction, which then allows the cells to take in the right amount of energy that's needed to perform at their maximum level of function, and release the expended energy out into their etheric body and send loving energy into the Cosmos, where it nurtures and regenerates the Whole. When the energy being sent into the universe is loving and creative, the energy being sent back energizes us and provides us with all types of opportunities. However, when energy is non resonant, the cells in our bodies become disorganized, and forget what their functions are, causing the body to feel dis-eased. Since water molecules change into dark, disorganized, and concentrated patterns, like mucus, when cursed at, and about 70% or more of every life form's body is water, imagine what these mutated water molecules are doing to the cells of every life form in our universe.

All life forms in our physical system have become distorted from their original form because of negative thoughts that created radioactivity in our universe, and hatred in the heart of humanity, but we can all become the perfect form that we were first born with through the power of the mind and the unity of the Whole. The mind is the power behind every creation and the movement of all energy. $E=mc2$ actually means, thought and emotion creates and moves all energy by the pulling force of feeling, and the pushing force of creative thinking, creating spiritual energy by the vibrations of movement through mediums like the manas of the mind, ether in space, water in oceans, and cytoplasm in cells, and when condensed, turns into matter. Every cell and atom is a universe in itself, and has its own consciousness. It is the thought that tells every cell in our body what to do and when the mind is full of doubt, fear, greed and hate, our cells start working improperly, or not at all as with cancer. Cancer, which is simply cells forgetting their function, prevents them from reaching cellular death and regeneration. The functioning cells reproduce more quickly to make up for the lost cells, creating an over abundance of cells in the system. These lost cells then travel to other systems of higher vibration in attempts to gain energy that will remind them of their function, known as metastasis, which of course invades another system. Since our mind is the source of all energy, it is our mind that can eliminate all cancer and dis-ease, but must be cleansed and brought to higher levels of consciousness.

All we have to do is teach everyone how to reclaim dominion over their own thoughts, and learn how to live their dream of life, not just surviving in the non life of evil by believing in the thoughts of others. We can eliminate the toxins from our bodies with natural organic herbs and foods, and by banning the use of all unhealthy products like flour, refined sugars, and animal products. Flour is simply grain stripped of all nourishment that fills us up when we're hungry, coats the intestines which prevents the proper absorption of nutrients, and makes us fat. Refined and artificial sugars cause people to be overly stressed resulting in many mental and physiological disorders like heart disease, diabetes, arthritis, depression, cancer and many more. Saturated animal fats actually prevent the usage of healthy omega fatty acids which are needed for cellular integrity, and many proteins found in animals are actually poisonous to the human body. We are not designed to eat meat, as evidenced by our inability to properly digest and metabolize these molecules, but were forced to in times of famine.

Humans and animals were friends and helped each other out until humans began to believe that they were superior to animals. It's the corruption of humanity that caused all famines, disasters, and separated all the kingdoms from the Creator, which of course is themselves. In truth all we need is pure air and water to survive.

People have been taught since they were a child that suffering is a natural part of life and that evil can control your thoughts, but the truth is that evil only steals your thoughts, and fools you into believing that you have no control over it. It causes you to procrastinate, becoming sedentary and forgetful, keeping you depressed, diseased and dying. People are constantly forgetting to do things, and failing to achieve what they dream of because their thoughts are influenced by this destructive energy that surrounds us, which unfortunately is separation from ourselves and desperation. Evil has also fooled people into believing that salvation comes from believing that outside forces, like God's will, Jesus' love, and influences from other spiritual leaders like Mohammed, Buddha, and Krishna, will save our souls and take us to Heaven and higher dimensions. The truth is God's will and love is the sum of everyone else's will and love, and can only be found in the Self, which is your own inner force. Unfortunately, religions have kept people focused on believing that God, Allah, and Jesus are higher forces and not your own inner force, causing people to feel that they are inferior and separate from them, and can only be part of them by physically dying. The Divine is desperately trying to reach every one of us and make us understand that we are all equally important, and must connect with our higher inner self before we can evolve to the next level, which is why we've been sent this Holistic plan of action.

The Divine, our mind, is constantly trying to reach us, our consciousness, like parents trying to find their lost children, but every time we make this connection, we quickly return to our external surroundings, and block out the internal thoughts. Even guru's and ascending channels can't continue to meditate when their physical form is being threatened. Every time you think of something that you've procrastinated, or hear your name being called but there's no one around, or more intensely, you experience a deja vu, vision, or pre-death awareness, you have managed to get through all the dark sludge in your mind and reach your conscious thought. When you reach your conscious thought you experience something magical and spiritual, frequently feeling like you are one with the universe, which you are, and wish you could stay there forever, but the belief in your external surroundings push you back from this dream state, and put you back into the fear state that we've been trapped in. If we could spend some time everyday reaching total relaxation and listening to our inner soul, we could uncover the truth about everything, by touching our centre. It is only then that we can start creating new life, and become the creators we once were. We can remember that we are the creator of our universe and express our place in the universe through time, space and form. It is possible for every single person to currently live their dream life in their dream house, designed and furnished by them, go to a job they love doing, and have lots of time and resources to experience all types of recreation and achieve inner connection, by implemonting the only true governance, the Holistic Governance. Everyonc in, on, and around Gaia deserves to have all the knowledge and resources necessary to live their lives to the fullest and in the moment, and expand their vibration to higher levels. Our goal in life is to define ourselves by creating an outer world, and learning that outer world through sharing, loving, and creating.

The foundation of this divine governance is presented in this book and describes a whole new way of life, called holistic living. The moment this new way of life is implemented, all natural and proven methods of healing will immediately be given to the people starting with those diagnosed with terminal and chronic conditions, including mental illness and poverty. This change will be a smooth and exhilarating transition because everyone is going to receive the vacation of their life time, and at the end will go to their new dream house in a neighborhood that feels like home, and to a job they enjoy doing, and contributes to the well being of the Whole. This vacation is actually a rehabilitation process where everyone will be healed of all disorders and deformities, assisted in finding their true interests and talents, and taught holistic ways of performing all activities of daily living, allowing them to design their perfect life. They will discover what form of employment they enjoy most and are most talented at, and taught the policies and procedures, job description, and documentation specific to their job, that will be uniform across the Nation, and hopefully the World. Not everyone wants big and fancy things. Many actually prefer to live in small and loving communities and commune with nature. If all the money being wasted and extorted were diverted to the funding of these changes, there would be an over abundance. It doesn't cost to live this perfect life, it just takes love, organization and commitment, and if we accomplish this by the end of 2012, the solar and cosmic energy being sent to us will not cause us to fragment. It will resurrect us! It will bring us all in alignment with ourselves, each other, and the Cosmos, allowing us to return to our original point of creation and the Creator to remember all lost and forgotten thoughts.

This magnificent book is first being delivered to the people of the United States, because as I mentioned, America has the expressions of all cultures and has a global position of power, but also because it is also on the brink of implosion. Just like with the great depression but ten times worse. No one will be safe from the desperately greedy and angry people, killing and stealing in attempts to survive. What is even more devastating is what's happening as a result of Gaia entering the photon belt which is causing disturbances in the electromagnetic fields, resulting in severe weather patterns and interferences with electronic devices and machines, causing wide spread blackouts, and bringing more chaos to the world. However, if the people of the world would bring balance and love back to Gaia, and repair the damage done to her chakras, this photonic energy will be enlightening, not destructive. Gaia is in the process of ascension which generates massive amounts of heat, and is the cause of global warming. This ascension will continue to heat the surface of Gaia as we enter the center of the photon belt, but if we are ascending our forms at the same time we'll join with this massive heat increase. However, when Gaia is in full ascension, those that are not resonating with her will burn up, regardless of how much money or power you have. Actually, it is those who are most consumed by evil that will combust first, and their souls will be lost forever.

Most Christians believe that as long as they believe that Jesus is their savior, he will protect them during this time, allowing all others who don't believe, to perish. What Christians must understand is what Christ actually taught. He taught above all else, God is Love, and has an eternal, unconditional love for all creations, and that we are all God's creations regardless of culture and religious beliefs. Therefore, it makes no sense that God, which is absolute unity, would want any part of humanity to be destroyed. It only makes sense that God wishes for every single person on, in and around Gaia to be healed and brought back into alignment, where they can ascend their vibration, and resurrect to the next level of spiritual evolution. Christ taught that God was not a separate entity, but the sum of us all, and that with true faith and love could cure all ailments, solve all problems, reawaken the dead from their pit of darkness, and transcend their physical body into a heavenly body through resurrection, also known as ascension. He taught that the only way to communicate with God, the Whole, is by living your life in the moment, not in the past or the future, and through prayer, which was not in a church or with a group of people, but alone and with nature. Church is simply a meeting place for people to join together and share their thoughts and ideas, and celebrate life together. Christ never taught that only he had the power of communion and resurrection, but that anyone who truly understood and believed in the truth would have those abilities. His disciples, who are considered the authorities of Christ's teachings, couldn't understand him because they believed the power of God was coming from him, and not themselves. The truth of God is that we are all God, and God can only be as healthy and happy as we are, so if we are sad, diseased and dying, then so is God. Heaven and Hell are states of mind and an environment that supports that state. Many people envision Heaven as being a Garden of Eden where all of Earth is beautiful, and all of life is loving and peaceful. The truth is this can only exist right here on Gaia, and only if humanity unites together along with all other kingdoms of nature. The truth is we have all become severely separated from the Divine, our own consciousness, causing us to become lost and on the verge of forgetting ourselves, being removed from The "Book Of Life"

Fortunately, we have ascending people and Gaia generating massive amounts of loving energy and sending it to all of us and our ancestors, which is why we are seeing an enormous increase in people looking for spiritual enlightenment. They have reached extremely high levels of consciousness and have regained our innate ability to communicate with Gaia and all her Kingdome. They have the knowledge and wisdom that will help design and implement the one true governance. Not a governance for one country, but for our entire world. This governance can be implemented easily around the world if those in power would do so, but if not, the American people are the ones with the resources and freedom to accomplish this. The American people are already contemplating the idea of forcing President Obama to step down because of the disorder that he has already brought, and the fear that he will bring our country into ruins, which is why now is the time to force a new election, and elect in a new governance that will improve everyone's lives, including those in organizations of crime, and positions of power. A revolution would be completely devastating to America because there are many gangs and militias ready to start wars at their leader's command, and if this occurs, the American military would retaliate with deadly weapons, and the American people would become barbarians. What's the sense in having dominion over nothing, and then to lose it all through spontaneous combustion during Gaia's ascension in <u>two years</u>? We are on the brink of creating World War III by the blatant acts of violence being committed by the United States military in countries like Iraq, Afghanistan, Korea, and more causing the world to hate Americans. We are very near the point of no return because this is our last chance for survival, and if we don't transform by 2012, we'll be too late.

This new form of governance, known as the Holistic Governance, is the only form of government that will save humanity. The energies of the Cosmos are arranging life events that will facilitate and support this incredible change by creating a division in America. This division is actually making people aware that everyone has the right to protection, support, and freedom. Even though America has extremely strong racial tensions, with militias in all races waiting for the moment to start their racial wars, America is a great country that has a strong sense of patriotism. Not patriotism for the American government, but patriotism for the idea of freedom and growth. Yes, the militias are very strong in their sense of superiority, but most of the people in the United States have learned to live with each other despite their differences. This is crucial because it will bring the American people the strength and compassion needed to make the greatest change in the history of humanity. These events have already started. A black, Muslim president, who has promised incredible change but demonstrates the same destructive decisions as all previous political leaders. Another important event is having political activists of Congress asking the American people to support their ideas against the president and democratic party. This has shown the people that they do have the ability to elect in a new form of government by electing people who have not been preselected by the governing party.

This year's elections are critical to getting the Holistic Government implemented, because the American government has become weakened and divided, but very dangerous because as they start to lose control over us, as is already happening, they will take more and more of our rights away and try to force us back into submission. We must act now before the secret society can regain their strong hold. Though the candidates chosen to run for election have already been chosen, it doesn't mean that they have to be elected. Anyone who is a citizen, with no criminal background can run for any Congressional seat and City Council seat, but they must have the knowledge and resources to run a campaign. Since these new leaders are diversified professionals, and not politicians, they will need the help of highly trained people, in highly classified areas, and the help of everyone donating to their campaigns. Once the Holistic Governance is established, campaigns will not be needed, because the people running for office will place their videos for public viewing, and all debates will be covered by the news. We must find these leaders of the world and elect them as our new and improved governance. They are people, who are experts in their field, and have committed their lives to helping others. They must be completely impartial, and believe with all their heart that Holistic Living is worth fighting for. They must be very wise and self assured because they will be going up against the most dangerous people in the world. The secret society is known for killing anyone who stands up against them, but if the new leaders stay surrounded by people they trust, they will be protected. These new leaders will be researching every area, including highly classified ones, to identify all the problems and areas of corruption, and finding solutions that will correct all problems. There are many underground organizations that are very knowledgeable, and will be available to assist them, and there are even members of the secret society, that are tired of living in a dying world and will believe that Holistic Living is the answer! They will be willing to disclose all areas of corruption, especially since they'll be able to submit everything anonymously. The Cabinet will investigate all claims, by using the help of all underground organizations, and anyone who is willing to help. We must elect these people for all governmental positions this year, and give them the help they need to perform the duties of their position, and get them all the information needed to identify all hidden problems, so they can find and implement the most efficient and cost effective solutions. They will hire other highly qualified professionals for their Executive Cabinets, and design new policies, procedures and standards.

If the secret society refuses to transform our world into a wondrous place and allow the people to use mass media for the coverage of candidates, everyone who feels they are qualified to be a holistic leader, and chooses to run for office, will need to make a video of a taped interview, stating all their qualifications, activity in public affairs, problems they've identified in their areas of expertise, and how they plan to solve them, then place them on the internet or in places like libraries and book stores for viewing. We need people in all major areas of healthcare, economics, media/telecommunications, social service, education,law enforcement/peer review/amnesty, energy conservation, agriculture, ecology, and land development.

Since there is a specific number of elected seats per state, each state will be designated a specific area of expertise to select their candidates from. They will be designated as follows: Maine, New Hampshire, Vermont, Massachusetts and Rhode Island-Healthcarc. New York, Connecticut, Maryland, New Jersey and Delaware-Economics. Pennsylvania, Ohio, Michigan, West Virginia and Virginia-Media/Telecommunications. North Carolina, South Carolina, Georgia, Florida and Alabama-Law Enforcement/Peer Review. Kentucky, Tennessee, Illinois, Indiana and Missouri-Social Service. Mississippi, Arkansas, Louisiana, Texas and Oklahoma-Energy Conservation. Wisconsin, Minnesota, Iowa, Kansas and Nebraska-Agriculture. South Dakota, North Dakota, Wyoming, Montana and Colorado-Education. New Mexico, Arizona, Utah, Idaho and Nevada-Ecology. Washington, Oregon, California, Alaska and Hawaii-Land Development. These were just chosen randomly, not because the states are more knowledgeable in those areas. This way, if the people do what they need to and elect a new Congress, based on the criteria listed above, the Congress will consist of experts in all major fields, which is the basic structure of a Holistic Governance.

The people choosing to run for office will focus sending their videos to the states that are designated to their field. They will be sent to major city libraries, and any other place that will screen them for inappropriateness, and present them for viewing, including the internet. The people, in a designated area, will then search for the candidates they feel are most qualified, and announce their selections publicly, which must be done before the election, so no two states elect the same people. The government has made it very difficult for anyone, who they have not nominated, to run for office, but with the help of political experts and donations from the people, it can be done! Every single person can contribute to making this happen, just don't be afraid to, because the consequences of not acting, will be much more horrifying, than anything the secret society can do to us. Since electronic elections are easily falsified, all votes will also be placed on paper ballots. The people can make sure that an honest election has been carried out by standing at the doors of all places of elections, count the number of people who enter, and compare them to the number of ballots. The ballots will then be counted by the people before any worker can leave, to assure no foul play. The results will be posted publicly. This may take days to weeks, but it will be well worth it. The people will elect a new Congress and City Council based on their general knowledge of all areas of expertise, their ability to stay calm in a crisis, face dangerous people and situations with confidence, and make holistic decisions that will protect and nurture the people.

Once the people are elected, everything changes, which normally causes disaster, but the people and Congress will be ready for it, and able to get policies and procedures implemented quickly and in a professional and effective manner. It won't be as stressful on people because everyone will be given plenty of time and assistance, to learn their new job descriptions. This includes being sent to school, which will be paid for, like doctors and nurses learning holistic medicine, teachers learning new teaching skills and true history, economists learning the new non-monetary economic system, and many more. Congress will have a very short time to design and implement these new programs, but with the help of the people, can do it. A Holistic Governance will supply everyone with the proper resources and opportunities to live holistically, and anyone who tries will prosper and soon start enjoying their jobs, families, and more importantly, themselves. It is guaranteed success, because it is based on the efforts and talents of everyone. The people will be the ones developing the new governance, therefore the governance will always support and protect the people. The newly elected officials, and hopefully President Obama, will then convert Congress into the National Executive Cabinet, which is the foundation of a Holistic Governance. Most of the world has been waiting and praying for their spiritual leader to save them, and take them to a beautiful place, but the only way that is going to happen, is by each of us making positive changes, and saving our world! Hopefully every country, including the secret society will want a Holistic Governance, and work together to create a holistic world, but if they don't, it will take the people to get this governance implemented, and to stop the evil that is devouring us. We must unite together and make these changes. The violence and destruction of Gaia and us, the true spiritual leaders, must be stopped before it is too late!

We must make the change right now! People say that we are past the point of extinction, but if evil succeeds in destroying our connection to Gaia, including those in higher dimensions, we'll lose the spiritual archives of our existence, because it was only through Gaia's unconditional love for all life, that she stored this spiritual knowledge, and it is only through the resurrection of all lost souls that humanity and those in higher dimensions can ascend! It is imperative that everyone understand, no matter what galaxy or level of dimension you're in, that we are ONE!!! Even those genetically created, referred to as the slave race, and races like the Reptilians, Sirians, and Anunnaki, are part of the Whole. We must all wake up from this horrible pit of forgetfulness and darkness, admit and forgive our transgressions, love each other for the truly beautiful life forms we are, and ascend back to our original state of being, and place of origin.

The Holistic Governance is for everyone and is founded on the strengths, imagination and compassion of every life form, and will design all the policies and procedures, standards and regulations, and job descriptions that will change every institution, organization and place of business into ones that will give everyone, no matter who you are, a real second chance! Everyone will learn how to live their life holistically. It is evil that keeps people of great wealth believing that dominion is a worthy cause. If the great wealth of the world would realize how incredibly happy their lives would become if their monies created a world where everyone around them, from those serving them, to their families and friends, were happy and respectful and fun to be around, they would have the opportunity to be the ones that saved us and all our creations. This governance belongs to the whole world and all other worlds in the universes, but it takes a starting point to make a drastic change, and the American people are that point! We must stop this descent of humanity that we've become trapped in.

This horrible descent of consciousness occurred from a simple oversight at a time when humans were experiencing life to the fullest. A few creative people decided to experience life in the physical but without one or more physical senses with the idea to experience a heightened awareness of certain senses. This was a natural stage of life, to experience the duality. However, they failed to contemplate the factor that every thought created was stored in the DNA of their physical body, and when they reproduced, their descendants were born without one or more physical senses and the understanding that it was simply a new experience of life. Through physical reproduction, the off springs consciousness is the consciousness of "I Am", being aware of the physical senses of the body. However, when it was time for the bodily senses to develop but didn't, these poor, unsuspecting, unborn children experienced the thought of being less than Whole. Just as the original thought of Self awareness exploded into new life of light, color, sounds, and bodily forms, the thought of Self being less than perfect, caused the Self to feel less love, and the more fragmented the Self became. Since the only goal in life is to unite what has been created, when the

Self was unable to create the missing senses, the Self was unable to internalize what was outside. They still had knowledge of these senses in their memories hoard, also known as unconscious and soul, but had no knowing of them because only through personal experience, through manifestation, is there knowing. If these unborn children were aware that it was just a new expression, they could have chosen to continue to live the expression given to them, or regenerate the missing sensory system and live life as being whole. Now that we understand how all thoughts change the energy patterns in our DNA, we will never again pass on negative thoughts to our descendants because it will be imprinted in our DNA that the absence of physical senses, or negative emotions are simply another expression of life and not a separation between Self and Self's consciousness. However, we must first repair what has been done and teach everyone how to clear these karmic attachments, raise their vibrations, and bring the outside in.

When these perfectly innocent children were born, they became the creators of evil, known as the Devil!! The descent of all humanity started with the birth of what should have been, pure and perfect babies. **Evil** is **Live** spelled backwards, and **Devil** is backwards for **Lived**, which is the true essence of their existence. The moment these children experienced this horrible separation and feeling of being lost, they stopped living. Yes their physical bodies continued to live, but only through cellular memory. Every cell in their body, except those involved with the sensory systems they were lacking, had their own consciousness and continued their function without the conscious guidance of the mind. However, this separation caused the children to stop making creative and loving thoughts, which is the pure essence of life. All they could think about was the horrible loneliness they felt when they could no longer communicate with the Whole through the language of ONE, and the fear of being cared for by a world they couldn't understand. Without being able to communicate telepathically or to see, hear, and feel the touch of their parents, they lost their ability to understand them. They learned to adapt out of the need for survival, but never understood the language of ONE. They never knew who they really were, or experienced the true powers of consciousness.

This horrible descent of humanity first occurred in an electric universe. Since the consciousness of one touches the consciousness of the Whole, when the innocent babies experienced separation from their inner self, the Whole felt the same separation! Not like the separation from nothingness, but the separation from Self. They all started descending in their level of consciousness causing them to forget their true loving and beautiful essence, and they started hating themselves for their error. However, it makes no sense to hate the electric life forms that created our descent because they were trying to bring growth to the Whole by experiencing something new. They were actually celebrated as being great creators until the moment the unborn babies became aware of their sensory loss. The parents tried to reach the baby's consciousness and show them that they had the power to create whatever they were lacking, but the babies couldn't understand. They hoped that the energy of a higher vibration was strong enough to reach through the darkness of these baby's minds, and show them the light that would lead them home. Home is your point of creation that defines your spiritual essence, and keeps you in alignment with the Whole. Om is also the original vibration of all life, and when sung, or spoken, with a yoga breath of life, creates the sound of home. However, the electric life forms became lost from their home and went looking to the magnetic universe for help. They hoped that the magnetic life forms could show them how to correct the devastation that occurred when their level of consciousness started becoming fragmented, and how to reunite the lost children of evil, and their descendants. They designed and implemented the plan that breeched the neutral barrier between universes, known as star gates, and entered through massive ships. They brought with them animals, plants, insects, and minerals they needed for temporary survival. Unfortunately, the magnetic world saw them as destructors, because their breech in the neutral barrier caused horrific disturbances and diseases, so the magnetic world didn't understand that they were actually coming in peace and hoping for help. The electric race was searching to find the answer that would reunite them, but when the magnetic world didn't have it for them, they became even more lost and were unable to find their way back to their own universe. They became stuck here and were unable to communicate with their world.

They knew that the regenerating powers of gold powder assisted the magnetic life forms with their ascensions, and planned to convert the magnetic energy of gold into an electric energy for them. However, they were unable to mine the gold because the magnetic chi made them extremely weak and sick, so they created a slave race of beings through gene splicing. The slave race, which were horrid monsters, then mined the gold and other precious metals and gems. When Gaia was depleted of gold and gems, her consciousness and the consciousness of all indigenous people started descending, causing them to see the electric life forms as superiors since they had the gold and the power.

The electric races then chose to stay in the magnetic universe and assume positions of authority, so they converted the magnetic suns into an electric sun by forcing the hydrogen atoms together, creating helium, which provided them with an electric chi. This radioactivity caused the cells of the magnetic life forms to combust resulting in aging, disease, and death so they moved underground, known as inner Earth. Through trillions of years, the DNA of every life form in this physical system has become mutated, carrying the errors of these ancestors, but with the help of Gaia, we can all find our original ancestry and return home where we belong. Gaia, along with all her kingdoms, ascending humans, and life forms throughout the Cosmos, are generating massive amounts of loving energy and sending it to all of us. All we need to do is unclutter our minds from negative thinking, and we'll start to feel all the love and understand all the creative thoughts, being sent to us. Everyone, including great spirits like Jesus Christ, Buddha, Krishna, Loa Tzu, Mohammad and others, have been trapped in this horrible pit of forgetfulness along with all of us. Yes, they are at incredibly higher levels of self awareness, but they too are unable to ascend because of all of us who have become lost and forgotten.

We lost our true powers of consciousness which are telepathy and dream weaving. Through telepathy, all you have to do is think of someone, and if they resonate with your thought you would immediately be there with them, not in body but in mind, and dream weaving is simply manifesting all your loving thoughts into a reality. Time is simply a reference point of the past, because the present is nil, and the future is simply our intentions. Teleportation and astro traveling are real. The mind can go anywhere it chooses to but in order to do so, you must understand the language of ONE, which can only be achieved by purifying your mind, body and consciousness. No one can use advanced mental powers for evil because the power only comes from loving thoughts. Movies and video games show evil people as having these powers but that's just to scare us from exposing evil for what is truly is, memory loss and separation. Evil has absolutely no power over a fully conscious mind, but can manipulate and control weak minds. To purify one's mind, body and soul, is to remember who we are and our purpose in life, and to forgive all the acts of self destruction throughout our entire ancestry, beginning with ourselves and our families.

Family is very important because it is the root of our physical existence, and we are the root of our descendants existence, and the descendants of our family members. Though our ancestries have been blurred with interbreeding, through our family tree we can find our original lineage of life. Everyone of us has been interbred, which occurred thousands of generations ago, even those who have currently remained within their tribe and culture. No one will know who their original ancestry is until we resurrect our physical form. The truth is that someone who is a top white supremacist may actually come from the Black Assyrian ancestry, and an Indian monk may be a descendant from the white Anu ancestry. Therefore, people who are prejudiced against a culture may actually be against their own ancestry. This horrible separation is actually the greatest gift we could all receive, because now we'll all have a knowing of each other, and not just an awareness of each other. Through our mistake, we have the ability to achieve the consciousness that we're not just part of each other, but that we are of each other. If we could succeed in resurrecting humanity out of this horrible pit of forgetfulness, we could resurrect our form and ascend to higher levels never reached before. We could create our own worlds, and experience life through the senses of all our creations, instead of accepting the universe as the will of others. You could be a bird, a whale, a human, a reptilian, an angel, or a planet, and anything you've ever imagined, including reaching the level of Christ's consciousness. You could also choose to stay as part of this consensus reality and accept the spiritual guidance from others in learning lessons of life. We could do whatever our hearts desire, but we must first join together and eliminate evil from all our lives by teaching our descendants this truth of life and how to live a healthy and happy life by manifesting our dreams into reality.

This devastating separation that occurred millions and trillions of Cosmic years ago created this Evil and is on the verge of actualizing itself, which is complete separation and darkness. This is not a force, it has no power over consciousness. It's only power is in number of people who have forgotten who they were and continue to manifest this nightmare that is leading us into extinction. This time of change, as spoken by all ancestors, and collaborated with current scientific evidence, has already begun and with time speeding up, the transformation of all life will occur in two years. That means if we don't stop the evil now, which everyone around the world must admit is horrifying, it will be much, much worse, and we will be the cause of the total destruction of our world, and the Universe. Already, we have beautiful and talented children being stolen around the world at alarming rates, becoming slaves to physical and sexual abuse. The world is currently at frightening levels of destruction, imagine the horror and pain in two years, when it really gets bad with people spontaneously combusting, and their souls being forgotten forever. The worse nightmare ever, is being all alone in total darkness, yet having the sense of an evil presence that is trying to devour you. This is real. This is what we are manifesting! All the evil happenings around the world have occurred many times before, beginning with the descent of consciousness, and will continue until we stop it or go extinct!!

You might be questioning my authority of knowing this truth, but it's not my authority. Incredible people like Albert Einstein, Leo Tolstoy, Frank Hatem, and channels like Lilliya, Oa, and Ken have given us this knowledge lovingly and freely. I am an average working woman and mother that had a spiritual encounter fourteen years ago and came to understand the creation of our total existence, the creation of evil, and the divine plan to reverse the damage that has occurred, which can still be corrected, but only if we act now. I've been afraid to get too much publicity, in fear that evil would harm me or my family, so I kept hoping that someone with authority and resources was given the same knowledge and would release their book to the world. Now that I've found this knowledge that supports my understandings on the internet, I feel supported in bringing this book to all the people. It is titled "The Resurrection Of Humanity" because only through our resurrection, the Whole, can we, the Divine, ever be saved. I am simply a vehicle for this spiritual knowledge which was sparked during my darkest hours of contemplating suicide. I experienced a connection to the Whole, to my Self, and afterwards I had a knowing of things that I barely understood, but recorded as best I could, and through the years have come to understand. It was the first time I had ever asked God to come into my life. Yeah, I went to church but church never brought me closer to God. I realized that it was because I was looking for God outside of myself in the minister, bible and church groups instead of looking inside myself with a quiet and focused mind that can be achieved through true meditation, or through a spiritual encounter like mine. I was so separated from myself that my life became a burden that I no longer wanted to bear. I suffered from a dissociative identity disorder known as DID, which can become more severe like with schizophrenia, multiple personalities and amnesia. A person will dissociate themselves from abuse in attempts to protect the psyche, which is the spiritual essence of the person. The psyche knows that they are perfect creations and will form other personalities to accept the abuse and become the abuse that they are being treated with and taught to believe as being their true self. Some accept this abusive life as their own, but fortunately I blocked it out, giving me the ability to see and hear the truth during my spiritual connection.

This spiritual connection began as a burst of light because in a flash night became day! I was surrounded by this brilliant light which seemed to encompass my total being. It was brighter than the sun, but soothing to my eyes, which allowed me to look even deeper. The more I looked, the more I could feel a presence all around me. There was a silence that reached into infinity that deafened even my own breath and heart beat. I felt as though I was floating in a vacuum. No earth under my feet, no breeze upon my skin, not even the fragrance from my perfume could I sense. I could move but there was no sense of movement or space around me. I became overwhelmed with emotions of love, hate, fear, joy, belongingness, loneliness, and much, much more. It was as if my mind was filled with visions from the lives of everyone. I saw and felt the horrors found in the depths of darkness, from the grips of power, greed and hate, but I also experienced the true joy of love and oneness with all life, and the intense intimacy between joined lovers. I came to know that world peace is possible, and a world of love, health, and growth is attainable. The power to change the world truly does exist!

Through a total darkness within the light, a cloudy haze began to appear. I was frightened of the unknown, but felt an incredible sense of peace. It was a being with a ghostly appearance. It had a humanoid like form but it kept changing the way it looked, from children to elderly, male to female, animal to plant, and insects to Earth's elements and creations. The dark center was like the pupil of an eye, which was a perfect mirror of everything outside it, and the light body was like the iris that reaches to the borders of infinity. I felt like I was the light body and the center was the spiritual essence of every life form created. I thought to myself, "what and who is this that I'm seeing"? I vaguely heard voices say, "Wake up! Please wake up so you can hear what is being said ." The sound of the voice was the most beautiful and musical sound I had ever heard, but also the cries and moans of suffering. It sounded like laughter, singing, languages, yells and cries from all the people, animals, plants, and even the wind. The voice didn't sound like it was outside of me. It was like it was enclosed in the same vacuum as me. All I could hear was my thoughts and the Messenger's, and felt this strong sensation coming from my center being. The same kind of feeling I got when I had a deva vue, a premonition, and when I first met my husband, but also a stronger feeling like when I did something wrong, and when I was hiding from someone chasing me. However, it was very soothing and erotic and spread throughout my entire body. I could feel every cell in my body start to tingle to the point where I felt like I had no body, only vibrations. I began to hear this ominous sound. It sounded like Om, with a long "o", which became louder and deeper, and as it did I began to feel this incredible vibration in the center of my body creating stronger pulsations. I started to hear the most amazing melodies, that formed words that I could understand, but they weren't like words I'd heard before. They were like different melodies in a song, but I could understand them. I later learned that this is the language of ONE, and by ascending my level of consciousness, I would be able to understand the different tones on a permanent basis. I thought this must be God but wondered which one, since different cultures believe differently.

Suddenly, everything went black. No light, no senses, no memory, not even the thought of being alive. A total nothingness until I suddenly felt something touching me, making me aware that there was something else other than me, and that I was the creator of this something else in attempts to separate myself from nothingness. I then had the thought to define this feeling through expression and understanding. I thought to express this feeling of touch, and became aware that I was embodied by spheres of pure spiritual energy, which was my outer world. I had the understanding that I was a divine feeling that just created a perfect body through divine thought, and together created a holism which was me, the creator, the self, the beginning of all life, time and space. This embodiment began as perfectly symmetrical spheres, that fit perfectly together to create a perfectly spherical embodiment. I created this illusion by creating lines of energy between each point of contact, and mathematically calculating the distance and angle from each other through their relativity. Since all sphere's were perfectly symmetrical, and were positioned side by side, creating another perfect sphere, the points of contact were all within the same singular plane, positioned in the direct center of each sphere, creating a concentric network of spiritual energy. This network of energy lines, known as meridians, formed the pattern of a hexagon, creating a singular plane of network within the center of all spheres. Each point of contact was then connected to the points adjacent to their adjacent points, forming the pattern known as the Star of David, and the Merkaba. The points of contact then sent energy lines to their opposite points of contact creating patterns like the five and seven point star, but most importantly, they all met at the exact same time, creating a center vertex point.

The only other feeling, other than the points of contact, was the pulling sensation coming from the centre, like having a gut feeling, or a buzzing in your head, a sense of density. When the meridians converged at the center vertex, the energy was sent to this center being of nothingness, but before they could reach the centre, they met with a barrier and the barrier was the periphery of the sphere. The energy encompassed the periphery by creating a perfect number of energy lines for every infinitesimally close area of the body, numbered 144000, sending all the energy along the periphery to the opposite point. Through all the mathematical calculations of points of contact and angular movements along the periphery, I became aware that the barriers were actually perfectly spherical bodies, that each body had six adjacent spheres touching them, and that the meridians were a network of energy lines in the center of, and along the periphery of each sphere of embodiment. When the meridians met at the opposite point of the spheres, they spiraled together, like thousands of DNA, forming a chord, and when they were pulled toward the centre, they formed a vortex, moving in the pattern known as the Fibonacci. This awareness of each other caused the peripheries of each sphere to become permeable, and when the chord continued the path toward the center of nothingness, the spheres were pulled together and overlapped each other, bringing their peripheries to the center point of each other and the centre, and crossing and pulling all center meridians toward the centre, creating the pattern of the flower of life. Each sphere joined together with their adjacent spheres gaining the awareness of each other and a strong desire to be one with each other. The spheres overlapped each other even further bringing their peripheries past the center point of the centre, creating the pattern of the lotus and tube of torus and the meridians created an intricate network of energy patterns within the center, like the patterns seen on media players visualizations.

I realized that my feeling was now the centre of my being, also known as the Source, the soul, the unconscious, and the id, and my thoughts were the embodiment of my being, also known as the Source of All That Is, the spirit, the conscious, and the ego. The sensation in my center being became extremely strong as my feeling of existence changed to the feeling of life through expression. I felt the force of my spirit explode pushing all my embodiment out in all directions, and at perfect angles from each other, with perfect degrees of magnitude, thereby maintaining a perfect spherical form of spiritual light. I realized that through my divine movement, and ability to mathematically calculate the relativity between all my thoughts of consciousness, that I just created a spark of pure spiritual electric energy, that created massive amounts of heat and cascaded an extremely bright light, for every new thought of movement. These new forms of thought, each created by a thought of consciousness, formed a new concentric circle around me, creating the same perfect spherical form, and number of new thought energy forms, I'll refer to as units of consciousness, or UC's. The new UC's then gave their energy to the thoughts of consciousness, pushing consciousness through their form to help create a new concentric circle of life. I continued to make new layers of life circles at an exponential rate, and the layers were infinitesimally close, creating linear propagations that appeared like light rays. When I carried the spiritual information from one layer of thoughts to the next one, the layer of thoughts were bigger, brighter and hotter, creating a Fibonacci growth factor, where the whole is always the sum of all preceding. My focus was along the periphery where I was constantly making new thoughts of life, so I was unaware of the thoughts that no longer had conscious attention.

Suddenly I felt the strong pull of my soul, shifting my conscious attention from my periphery where I was continuously creating new mathematical calculations and movements of energy, to my centre. At that moment, when I stopped creating and moving forward, I looked back at my previous thoughts and realized that I had stopped thinking about my thoughts the moment I created new ones, and that without conscious attention they lost their heat and brilliance of light, making then colder, darker, and slower, allowing them to be pulled back along their propagations towards the centre, through a medium that was created by their heat and light particles of creation, known as space, the sea of mind, and inertia. When the first layer of forgotten thoughts reached the centre, stopping their descent, the second layer touched them. This beautiful touch created amazing feelings of closeness and the desire to caress, embrace and join together with every other thought energy form. This immediate attraction between the points of light caused them to become permeable to each other allowing them to diffuse through each other's peripheries and intertwine with each other's energy. When their peripheries met with the center of an adjacent sphere they created a spark of energy that generated a warm and loving heat.

The heat made my points of light start moving faster, but instead of away from each other, they stayed connected at their peripheries, causing them to rotate around each other, creating a friction energy and magnetism, which created sparks of a warm colorful light, tone, and vibration. Though I had no physical senses, I knew the colour was red, the tone was Om (long O), the musical note C, and the vibration was like a delta brain wave, the dream state. This force began pulling the points of light to the center, which is what changed my consciousness along the periphery, to the centre. When all points of light reached the centre, becoming part of this rotational, and perfectly symmetrical collection of magnetic light, moving around a force void of any light, creating the appearance of a black hole, they all stopped moving. At this point I became aware of every single unit of consciousness having their own unique spiritual essence, along with the spiritual essence of my total body, making us all ONE. This eternal and unconditional desire to be one with the whole, known as divine love, created an absolute knowing of every unit of consciousness. Through this absolute knowing I was able to create a prefect recollection of each thought form, known as memory. I had memory of their exact location at the point of their creation, their size, and their position among all the others. I became aware that this memory was created by the eternal, unconditional love that was created by touching and holding, giving me the ability to recreate the spiritual essence of every thought I had ever created. I had the understanding that I was not just the observer, but that I was the Creator.

Suddenly I burst out in all directions, but this time I was points of light with attached memory, appearing as half light and half dark. Each point of light had a black memory spiraling around it, giving the appearance of the yin/yang symbol, with a red aura around it. Each point of light/ dark, or thought/memory energy form was released in the exact direction and sequence as first created. When the energy forms, or units of consciousness, reached the outer boundary of my first expansion, I became aware that movement was not just mathematical calculations, but also patterns. I continued to move along linear propagations, as the energy forms created spiraling and expanding walls, like cones, which spiraled out at the same rate as the formation of the units of consciousness, the Fibonacci number. The patterns in the walls were like visualizations on a music media player. I then reached a point of maximum expansion where I had created another perfect number of units of consciousness along linear propagations, numbered 144000, and again, returned to the centre. I had a profound feeling of Self admiration for having created such incredibly beautiful patterns of energy. This time the color of light was orange, the tone was oo (long u), the musical note D, and the vibration was like the brain theta waves.

I then became aware that I had a choice to create more thoughts and ideas, or simply exist as memory, known as free will. I became profoundly aware that only through growth is there life and only through life is there future. I learned that self discipline was required to continue my growth, so I expanded out creating more intricate patterns of energy with an orange aura. I again reached a maximum range of expansion, creating another perfect number of patterns, numbered 144000, and again returned to the center where everything became ONE. The reunion created a yellow colour, the tone "aah" (short O), the musical note E, and the vibration like theta-alpha brain waves. I became aware of a strong sense of trust knowing that I had the discipline to always create more, known as living. I again burst out creating more energy patterns, each time following the same paths as originally created and becoming more and more intricate as I created new paths, or Taos. I became aware of the concept of learning as I created new patterns while remembering the past ones. I realized that I was creating the future, known as Dance of Life, through intentions to create new patterns and energy, and regenerating them through memory. I contracted after reaching the perfect maximum point of expansion and returned to the centre sharing all information with the memories hoard. The magnetic energy created a green colour, a tone of "aay" (long a), the musical note F, and the vibration like alpha brainwaves. I then became aware that I could organize my intentions into plans of action.

My intentions to always grow and become more, developed the idea of perpetual growth by creating life forms, in the perfect image of myself, that had the ability to create their own Dances of Life, and these creations then becoming Creators themselves, continuing the Dance of Life indefinitely. I returned to the Centre with much stronger feelings of love because of my wisdom and dedication. The loving magnetic energy created the colour blue, the tone "ee" (long e), the musical note G, and alpha-beta brainwaves. This feeling of self idealization caused me to burst out again, giving me the energy and insight to create a divine plan of self recreation. Not just expanding myself, but giving everyone of my thought energy forms their own awareness of self and ability to create their own dance of life, expanding my one dance of life, to an exponential number of life dances. I again returned to the centre and my understanding of self actualization and self love created the colour indigo blue, the tone "mm", the note A, and the beta brain waves. I then burst out again with the awareness that by releasing my thoughts from conscious direction, meaning that each new thought/ memory form would be on their own, they would have to be released in perfect alignment and in order of their vibration to keep their position of creation. I realized that every new level of creation was given their own unique spin around the Whole when their vibration was created, causing each to rotate around the preceding one, and when the remembered thoughts reached their maximum point of expansion, they formed an aurora around them as the new creative thoughts continued to expand out in more intricate patterns. I also realized that every time I expanded out, I remembered every thought I had created and their patterns of energy, and when the thoughts of one vibration reached the aura to the next vibration, the pathways were in perfect alignment. This perfect alignment is held by memory, therefore by giving every thought/memory energy form memory of all preceding thought/memory energy forms, they would stay in alignment with each other. That way, no matter how fast or slow an individual energy form expanded, they would always know their pathway back to the Centre where they can share all their thoughts and memories with the memories hoard, and learn about all the other energy forms that had returned and shared their experiences.

I learned in this last expansion of myself, that I had to be completely focused and disciplined in maintaining a total consciousness of the creation and movement of all thoughts as I released them into a world of unknown. I returned to my Centre where the highly magnetic energy created the colour of violet fire, or pure white, which is the unity of all colours, the tone "nnggg", the note B, and gamma brain waves. I then became aware that there were not only seven distinct vibrations, but that each aura had their own vibration, and instead of seven vibrations, there were thirteen, and that each vibration moved the linear pathways in a vortex pattern, that led to the aura of the same pathway of the preceding lineage. Every unit of consciousness had two vortexes that spiraled down to the vortex of the UC's before and after it, creating a ground zero between them. It is at the point of ground zero that knowledge and memory is exchanged. I then felt this immense force from within my embodiment push my entire being out in all directions, just like with my first expansion of consciousness, but this time instead of my thoughts being a continuation of all preceding thoughts, they each had their own awareness of self, with their centre being my consciousness, and their alignment of creation. They became aware of their own spiritual essence, which was their unique vibration and position of alignment. This was as exponential number of units of consciousness, or particles, and my aim was to keep them all together as they each created new life through manifestation and re-creation.

I then realized that I had created a physical universe, allowing me to experience all these incredible movements of energy through the emotions and senses of every physical body created. It started with nebulas that formed into gaseous planets, based on their vibrations, then minerals that formed into rock planets, stars that formed the intricate networks of energy that aligned the chakras in the universe, suns that were colorful and stored the energy, comets that gathered and delivered energy where needed, natal planets that supported new biological life forms, and moons that stored the memories of their planets. I saw clouds form around natal planets, creating water that then created an algae that covered the minerals. The algae and minerals then formed into vegetation and single cell organisms. The organisms then grew into insects, animals and eventually homosapiens. They had different appearances like, elves, leprechauns, and other life forms that have gone extinct, and of course, human beings. They then transformed into ghostly appearances with wings, known as angels, and then pure energy. I became part of this pure energy, and began to understand with my limited knowledge of science and spiritualism, that God is not a separate entity directing and watching over our lives, but the consciousness of us all. Everything we think and feel, God thinks and feels. We govern the movement of God, because we, the descendants, are the periphery of the Whole, and how we think and feel determines the energy being produced by the Whole. I learned that God is pure consciousness, and the beginning of this consciousness was the beginning of all time, space, and energy. The awareness of being alive and having a pure and perfect spiritual essence, known as the Self, Spirit, Source and Consciousness, that manifests universes. I then understood that I was one of these magnificent creations and that my purpose in life was to evolve through these twelve stages of self development, reaching the thirteenth stage of recreation, but because of the descent of humanity, I was at the first level of simply being alive and needing to learn how to identify, love, respect and nurture myself. I also remembered being given information on how to design and implement a governance that will save humanity, and bring unity to the Whole. The Holistic Governance!!

The Holistic Governance consists of three major components. The Executive Cabinet, which will exist at the local, state and national levels, the Peer Review Process, and the Amnesty Period. The Cabinets, will consist of experts from each major field such as healthcare, education, economics, and ecology, and could be a doctor or nurse, dean or professor, and so on. The title is not as important as the person's knowledge and level of commitment. The Executive Cabinet will be formed at the local level in every community, and will be represented by the Cabinets at the state and national levels. Every cabinet member will have equal responsibility and value. No one will have control over someone else. Every year there will be an election, starting with the National Executive Cabinet, the second year the State Cabinets will be elected, and the third year, the Local Cabinets, in which every Cabinet will have a three year term. Only the original State and Local Cabinets will be appointed by the National Cabinet, the first year because it will be those we elect that know who is best in assisting them with the development of the truly divine governance. After that, they will be elected by the people, who are the ones that know who has served them best. The elections will be held on Halloween, actually the first full moon following the fall equinox, because this point in time has been established as a day of high spiritual energy, and is a time where the physical and spiritual worlds are closest. It will become the day to celebrate our new way of life, through annual elections of The Holistic Governance! Every election will be recognized as a national and spiritual holiday because government and spiritualism are one. It will still be a day for costumes and parties, and people receiving gifts, but there will be no promotion of evil, because by then there won't be any evil since everyone will have been healed and enlightened. Each Cabinet will form their own committees of experts, that will assist them in developing all the job descriptions and policies and procedures that will correct the problems and ensure the proper implementation of programs in all organizations and businesses. Until the rehabilitation process is complete, all programs and actions of people will be evaluated on a constant basis to ensure that the problems are being identified, and that everyone and everything is functioning properly. This system is called the Peer Review Process and will be part of every organization and business. It will also be part of the personal lives of everyone. Everyone's behavior will be monitored to ensure the proper adjustment to a new environment. Even the Cabinets will have the public as their Peer Review, in which any member can be dismissed at any given time with just cause. The Amnesty Period is essential to the success of any change. It is a period of time which allows for everyone to admit all their wrong doings, expose all illegal businesses, and release all top secret information, without receiving punishment. Everyone will receive all the opportunities and proper rehabilitation needed to find what is right for them, and help them in converting their businesses into holistic ones, which will bring happiness to everyone. Everyone, including the secret society, will receive holistic rehabilitation, with no exceptions. Remember, everyone, except those who have already ascended to higher levels, needs holistic rehabilitation. Every method known to heal and increase consciousness will be utilized, and everyone will receive everything they need to achieve their dream life. The number of local cabinets will be based on the city's population and resources, and will create and govern a specific Community Center.

Community Centers are establishments that will unite people into communities, by providing total care for everyone within a specific designated area. Large cities will have several Centers, that will be zoned according to population and resources. They will also be "big brother" to all rural areas. Every community will have a major hospital, schools with professional staff and nationally approved equipment and resources, stores stocked with healthy and high quality products, recreation centers, parks, and much more. Everyone, no matter who you are will be assigned to a specific Community Center. The Community Center will become the employer and supplier for everyone. There will be no money. Through the rehabilitation process everyone will learn that money is simply a device that establishes superiority over inferiority, and once the rehabilitation process is complete, we will all become equal, which is our true natural state. The idea of no money is actually very simple. If you can go to a business and get what you need, whether it be food, furniture, car, healthcare, and even controlled substances and sexual entertainment, and not have to pay for it, why would you need money? Everyone will have a job that provides service to others, and the Community Centers will ensure that the jobs required to meet the needs of their communities are filled. Yes, at first during the transition phase the Cabinet will have to ensure that everyone is assigned to a Community Center and supply everything the people need and desire. There will be a maximum of what you can receive, but once we're rehabilitated, we won't need to be monitored. Everyone will be a contribution to the Whole by providing service, creativity, and love, and everyone will be known by the Whole for their talents, hard work, and compassion.

The rehabilitation process will begin with the chronically ill, elderly, and incarcerated people, then anyone who is diseased, disfigured, or poor, eventually reaching everyone. They will first go through a diagnostic process, discovering every ailment they are inflicted with, and their original vibration, meaning their true ancestry. This is important because Gaia has different areas of vibration that will help heal those that resonate at that particular vibration. Remember, everyone has been distorted from their original vibration, but their spiritual essence can never be altered, so through soul testing, they can discover their true vibration. Everyone, no matter who they are have some genetic trait from another culture. As we start raising our vibration back to our original vibration, our cells will also change their patterns, recreating our original body. Through the law of attraction, if you are attracted to foods, architecture, and language of a culture, then you probably are a descendant of that culture. This rehabilitation process is essential in finding our true self and our way back home, which means becoming aligned with our universe. Everyone will be assisted in discovering what their true desire in life is, whether it's a nurse, architect, farmer, teacher, shaman or homemaker. They will design their dream home, furnished with what they love most, and choose where they want to live, but only in areas that resonate with their biological form. Everyone that has been healed will regain their abilities of telepathy, telekinesis, and teleportation, therefore there will be no secrets, nothing to hide. Powers of the mind can only be awakened by the love of the soul, which is why negative thoughts have no power, only the ability to manipulate other weak minds. Since evil is actually memory loss, when everyone is reawakened, and remember who they truly are, evil will no longer exist. Every Center will be governed by a Local Cabinet, who will teach everyone their new job descriptions, policies and procedures, and regulations that have been created by the Executive Cabinet. They will ensure the proper implementation of the peer review and amnesty processes, and the accurate reporting of all findings. Everyone with talents will be discovered, and recognized in all the arts. Artificial creations will not be allowed to be advertised as originals. You will not be allowed to use equipment to change the sound of your voice, or reproduce paintings, and sell as authentic. Art, and recognition of its creation, belongs to the artists around the world, not some businessman. Art is meant to be shared worldwide, and it is the artist who deserves full benefit. The evil in our world has taken art away to keep us depressed. People are of equal value and will be given every opportunity to discover their true interests and talents and reach their full potential!

Hopefully those who have millions of dollars, and have every material thing they've ever wanted, will actually find joy in bringing happiness to others. There is a very big difference between wealthy and rich. One can be wealthy in the most valuable things in life which are health, love, knowledge, and positive memories, or rich with money and possessions. Riches keep you focused on them instead of life which is learning new things, socializing with others, and most importantly, spending quality time with your loved ones. This is depicted in a saying from the Bible, "It is easier for a camel to go through the eye of a needle, than for a rich man to enter into the kingdom of God". Riches, if not used for the benefit of the Whole, will become evil and devour your life. You may have the illusion of happiness because everything you think you want, you can buy, but the things that your mind, body and soul need, can only be achieved by living holistically. Every business will be converted into productive and healthy ones, and people who have businesses that provide adult products and entertainment will be able to continue in private, and heavily monitored communities. Since most of the world has been touched by the plague of hate and greed, rehabilitation programs and facilities will be abundant. The military will change their job descriptions into ones that will cleanse the earth, clean up the neighborhoods, and build recreational areas for all the people. They will protect only the land that they reside in, which includes putting out large fires, hydrating dried up areas, and drying up flooded areas. They will be removed from all foreign lands because every country has the right to be governed by their own culture and not by a foreign government. Therefore all embassies must be closed down, and if any person or company wishes to stay there, they must denounce their citizenship with their country, and pledge allegiance to the country they reside in. This does not mean that tribal, or native people can't live as their ancestors did, because they will be given all the resources and land needed to do so. They live by the laws of nature, which is love and respect for all, and it is they, the indigenous people of Gaia, who are eager to bring health back to Gaia and form the new consensus reality of unity and peace. Every country wanting to develop a Holistic Governance will receive the resources to do so, but their actions will be monitored closely to ensure that they are doing things correctly.

We must bring forth the true leaders of the world to implement this incredible governance that is guaranteed success and will save our world and the Cosmos. We can't just dream of a happy and healthy life, we must live it! We know that everyone, no matter how evil and cruel they have been, have the potential to stop the evil in their life, and live a life full of love, health and productivity, if given the proper education and resources. If everyone was surrounded by people behaving in a polite, professional and caring way, families would become friends, neighbors would become communities, and countries would become allies. Everyone has differences and if all differences were respected instead of feared or hated, the world could achieve peace and find new discoveries beyond their wildest dreams! The only way to teach people how to live right and enforce positive changes is by the people forcing their governments to adopt and implement The Holistic Governance!

The first step in creating a Holistic Governance is to elect the Executive Cabinet who will then choose their cabinet members. They will design the regulations, policies and procedures, and job descriptions for every organization and facility, and the rehabilitation process for every living being. The focus of the Holistic Governance is to find problems and fix them, which includes people. The process of helping people realize their problems, and teach them how to solve them, is called rehabilitation. Rehabilitation is the changing of lives into holistic ones, and the first ones to receive assistance will be the homeless, disabled, elderly, and imprisoned. This starts by supplying people with homes that are bright and full of healthy energy, complete with all the essentials of life, and chosen comforts, including a temporary live-in trainer if needed, and jobs that are best suited for them, as determined by self examination, and aptitude testing. When someone's name comes up for evaluation, everyone in their circle of family and friends, will also be evaluated. That way family and friends can be rehabilitated together. Everyone will be given all the time they need to complete the rehabilitation process, allowing them to move into their dream home and start working at the job that's right for them, or continue their schooling. Anyone keeping a good grade point average can stay employed as a student, just as parenthood is a job. Bad credit and reputations will be erased, and given a clean slate. Everyone will eventually be evaluated, including the richest of the rich, the poorest of the poor, and the highly secured officials, and all will be treated equally. The homeless woman, who sells sex for a living, deserves as much respect as a president of a large corporation. She may be very smart and talented, who with the proper resources, could become a world renowned artist or scientist. There is so much talent that has been buried under all this evil, that if it was discovered and allowed to flourish, the world would be full of amazing people. Rehabilitation will discover the good in people, and support all their interests and talents. It will be part of nearly everyone's life, and anyone who harms themselves and others, will receive special therapy. Everyone will learn how to live holistically, which includes eating healthy foods and drink, proper exercise which includes yoga, meditation/prayer, and healing techniques like massage, reflexology, aromatherapy, and many others. Anyone who fails to respond positively with conventional methods, will be placed into secured rehabilitation centers. They will receive holistic care, and hormonal and psychological treatments. Everyone charged with a crime, no matter how insignificant, will be evaluated by a Peer Review Committee within their own community. That way the people will be more aware of the person's record and actions, allowing them to decide the most appropriate form of rehabilitation, and be there to see if the person makes positive changes. Anyone who is sentenced to a secured center will be placed in their own community, where they will do community service for those they betrayed. Everyone's actions will be of public record, including the governance. There will be no top security in the Executive Cabinet or the law enforcement. War has always been to take from others without their consent. It has never protected anyone. There will be no wars! If someone or militia tries to overcome others, the law enforcement will stop them by using methods known to temporarily immobilize them, and place them into appropriate secured rehabilitation centers or camps. There will be no political amnesty. If a person or militia, enters a country and commits a crime, they will be apprehended by the law enforcement, evaluated by the peer review process, and assigned to a rehabilitation center or camp. Consultation with their country will determine proper placement. The actions of everyone will be monitored, and this includes police officers, judges, and also security guards who will become rehabilitation workers. Organizations like the CIA and FBI will become members of the Law Enforcement or Peer Review Committee, following all the set standards and disclosing all information. As people progress through the rehabilitation centers, they will be placed into halfway houses, or previous homes and monitored until they demonstrate complete rehabilitation. Everyone will be expected to treat each other respectfully, and their belongings responsibly.

A Holistic Governance is designed to restore neighborhoods where children are safe to play and families can join together with friends for fun and relaxation. Communities will provide a sense of unity among the people because the environment will be conducive to their vibration. People have the right to live around people who have similar beliefs and values, where they can have a sense of belongingness and freedom. Some believe that segregation causes racialism, but desegregation caused racial riots. It is the anger in people, blaming others for their problems that cause racialism. Everyone is a child of God/Brahma/Self and loved equally. People will be able to live as their ancestors did with the same kind of housing, clothing, foods and entertainment. This is particularly important in the country of the United States, where they have citizens from every culture, though everyone will be encouraged to return to their land of resonance, provided the world joins together. Every community will define their boundaries with their Community Center, and everyone living in an area that is not resonant with them, will be given all the assistance to relocate to any resonant area of their choosing. Private Communities that are designated as adult communities will have stores for controlled substances like tobacco, alcohol, marijuana, cocaine and more, with prostitutes for both sexes, but only until rehabilitated. Everyone entering will be monitored for the amount of consumption of controlled items, which will be placed on national records, and if in excess of allowed amounts will receive immediate rehabilitation. Harmful substances like tobacco, alcohol, and poisonous chemicals, will be phased out as the people are rehabilitated, but substances like hemp, poppies, peyote, mescaline, and white gold powder, when used holistically, can give you energy, confidence, creativity, and self awareness, along with numerous medicinal purposes. The only places where controlled items and services will be purchased is in state stores and casinos located in adult communities, or prescribed by a Holistic physician. There will be no private communities that can hide their actions. Surveillance technology can monitor the actions of anyone, which will be governed by the Law Enforcement Committee. However, they may only monitor a person or business with just cause and as part of rehabilitation. No one, not even the Cabinet will have the authority to monitor people without them knowing about it, except in public. There will be cameras everywhere and anyone acting inappropriately and breaking the law, will be dealt with immediately. Every community will become a place where people can go to school or work in a relatively stress free environment. That is, no one's behavior will be allowed to distract, intimidate, or ridicule anyone. People need to be happy in their jobs, and children need to feel safe and nurtured in their schools.

All schools will implement the most effective means for learning and will be uniform among all schools. This includes all patented programs known to facilitate learning. Learning is not just for the rich, but for all. Schools in private communities can have more advanced resources and offer more programs, but must adhere to the same standards as all other schools. Every school will receive high quality resources like computers, hands-on projects, pools, sporting equipment, and products for all the arts. The curriculum will teach basic language and ways of life from all cultures, the language of ONE, and the truth about thought, love and magnetic energy. They'll be taught how to care for themselves and their future families in a holistic way. Everyone, starting at elementary levels, will explore the arts and athletics, to help discover interests and talents. The purpose of school is to find the interests and talents of everyone and prepare them for independent and holistic living. College and vocational schools are continued education and will be provided to everyone who wishes to attend, as long as a specific grade point average is maintained. Schools will become enjoyable for students, and rewarding of all their efforts. Parents should not make their children feel stressed by learning earlier and more than others. Let them learn at their own pace and choose their own interests. Every child will be provided the resources to learn, from birth on up. If a child says they see ghosts, or can do special things, believe them, be proud of them, and encourage them to explore and expand all their talents. The sole purpose of life is to grow by learning and experiencing new things, and loving all that they do. Learning should always be fun and exciting, just like people's jobs should.

People choose a career because they believe they will enjoy doing it, but when their place of business is stressful and depressing, people learn to hate what they do. Places of employment can easily become much nicer places by using condensed and uniform documentation, having healthy working hours, a clean environment, and not allowing disruptive or unprofessional behavior from anyone. A person could move from one state to another, and as long as they remain in the same area of expertise, they will have the same policies and procedures and documentation. All standards and policies and procedures will be specified by the Executive Cabinet. Every employer will designate a Peer Review Committee to continuously monitor for inappropriate behavior, and faulty areas in programs and equipment. Everyone will have annual competencies to ensure their proper skills and knowledge. Anyone failing will be given the assistance to regain competency, or move to another area that is more appropriate to their interests and talents. People need to feel respected by their peers, and feel good about themselves and their careers. Everyone will have to follow the set standards and policies and procedures as determined by the Executive Cabinet.

Money will become a concept of the past. Community Centers will employ everyone, ensuring that all areas of necessity are employed, and that everyone employed be given all the resources needed to start and continue their holistic living. Everyone will receive top quality products that will meet their needs for many years, and opportunities to turn in their belongings for new ones as their interests change. Everyone will be given a job appropriate for them, or given the assistance to start and maintain a business. Employers must have just cause to dismiss someone from their place of business, in which case they would receive rehabilitation, and placed into a more suitable job. There will be no mandatory overtime. Everything more than 40 hours will be volunteer. There will be however, mandatory vacations, either one week every three months, two weeks every six months, or four weeks yearly, starting from the date of hire. No employee will be allowed to work more than 60 hours a week, or 12 hours in a 24 hour period, and emergency services must take at least one hour recovery period after each major call. Employers must stop stressing people out, especially themselves, with long and hard working hours and high staff-client ratios, and start getting them healthier by providing healthy foods and drinks, and a place to exercise and relax. People will work harder and better when treated holistically. If the goal of business owners were to provide services or products that would benefit the lives of others, their business would flourish, and everyone would be healthier and happier. The people should also be able to enjoy their life after retirement, by continuing to have the same resources needed to continue their holistic living. People deserve to enjoy their life just as much as when employed, yet have all the time to do things they've always wanted, but was too busy. People who become injured or diseased will receive 100% of their resources until healed, and with holistic healthcare, it won't take long. No one will be allowed to lay around and utilize the Community Center's resources. That is not Holistic Living. Everyone has a purpose and can give a contribution to the Whole, whether it's art, performing arts, teaching, healing, farming, or producing products. We all have a talent that needs to be shared with the Whole.

The Cabinets will decide together, the most effective means of establishing a Holistic way of life. Every area of expertise touches all other areas, and every member must take into consideration those effects when developing their standards, job descriptions and policies and procedures. The Healthcare Committee will identify the most natural and effective treatments for all diseases and disorders. Gaia has provided everyone with herbs, foods, metals and minerals that will cure all ailments, which includes the use of air, water, earth and limited sun, because they all have healing properties. Holistic medicine is the proper application of only natural herbs and foods, healing techniques and exercises, and the elements, which includes stones like crystal and lithium, and also magnets. Mainstream medicine practitioners typically refuse to use naturopathic medicine to help diagnose and heal, but they will be required to learn it, and practice holistic medicine. A large percentage of the world uses pills for quick fixes to their problems, but health cannot be obtained through pills. Pills can only control acute conditions and prolong unhealthy living. Only through holistic living can one be truly healed. Psychiatric disorders can only be corrected by finding the source of the patient's disassociation, removing them from the source, and providing them with holistic care. If a person feels protected and loved, they can face the secrets that haunt them and accept them as a part of life that no longer has control over them. Haunting memories can be forgiven and accepted as a life event that teaches us and assists with our ascension. People who have blocked bad memories can learn how to remember them in a holistic way that allows them to face them with courage, and forgive them with compassion. There will always be times when we make a mistake, but if we learn from the experience, ask for forgiveness from anyone we've harmed, and continue to live our new and positive life, we will live in our inner self and reach higher levels. All anyone has to say, at any given moment is, "I'm not going to let anyone hurt me anymore, including myself, because the past is the past, and I've been given a new chance for life, by teaching me to trust in myself, love with all my heart, soul and mind, and live in the present". If we fill our minds and souls with the true desire to find enlightenment, regardless of a bad past, we can achieve what great spiritual leaders have, and at the time of our passing into rebirth, "Judgment Day", we'll be able to face all our bad memories, and remember that we are a special and loving spirit, and can choose to be reborn into any life of our choosing. If evil memories remain unresolved, we will feel guilty for the harm we've caused ourselves and others, seeing only the darkness, and being reborn into a lower level of consciousness. We have been in the dark far too long. It's time we learn how to heal ourselves through rehabilitation and join with the everlasting light of life!

To rehabilitate any disease or disorder, we must understand the limbic system and the chakras. The limbic system is the oldest system in the body, which contains the structures that house and govern all emotions and long term memory, which are the only things that go with us into our next life. It is the physical system that connects us to the Cosmos and is completely dependent on the energy in the chakras to function. Evil energy pollutes the chakras which leads to disease and death. The fornicate gyrus, located in the limbic system, releases chemicals that allows for sexual stimulation. This occurs when people are in their twenties, not teens. It is a stage of development where people establish their self identity, and have the emotional stability to develop successful and holistic relationships. Having sexual relations with others should be illegal until the adult age, just like consuming controlled substances and voting. It is not natural to have sexual desires for others early in life. The teenage years are for bonding, not intimacy. The greed and lust of "Man" forced people into unnatural relationships by raping them as children, or teaching them to have intercourse at an early age. Anyone who feels uncomfortable about masturbation and oral sex, are not ready for a sexual relationship. Intercourse should only be used when the couple is ready for parenthood, and women should stop taking birth control since it is toxic to them. Child abuse is so severe, that a lot of people started sexually abusing their children as babies. They play with the infant's genitals, while the infants suck on theirs. I know this is shocking to hear, but it is happening all around the world. Babies are naturally stimulated, by the touching of their genitals because it feels good, and will suck on anything that is placed in their mouths, but people that are driven by greed and lust, become sexually aroused, and convince themselves that since the children are theirs, they can do whatever they want. But then, when these disturbed people feel that the child is old enough to handle the size of their genitals, or other objects, the sexual activity changes from being playful, to painful and devastating. Children can't understand why this is happening to them, or have any way to stop it, so they disassociate their psyche from their abuse, like I did.

Depending on the individuals defense mechanisms, they develop disassociated disorders like schizophrenia, DID, manic-depressive, obsessive-compulsive, or borderline personalities. Some victims turn into rapists and murderers, because of all the evil that was forced upon them as a child. They are angry, conniving, and dangerous because they develop a partnership with evil, being fooled into believing that the more control they have over others, the more power they'll receive. However, true power only comes from your inner self, which only happens when you become one with yourself. We have movies that show people being obsessed by the "Devil", which in reality most of us are. It's not some monster, it's a darkness that guides and governs our lives. Even if you believe in the Divine, your life is being influenced by evil. We must face this Devil by admitting to ourselves and others, all the lies and abuse that has been part of our lives. We can look at the truth with bravery because we know that the truth will set us free, and no matter how bad our past has been, there is a new life waiting for us, because we're the ones who can create it. We must eliminate the evil in our lives by living holistically. Get out and meet your neighbors, and get involved in community activities! People are drawn to an area in which they establish their homes, because of the energy they feel from others. Therefore, they have the basic instinct to like their neighbors, but evil encourages people to isolate themselves and to not trust anyone. In order to save our world, we must break away from this dissociative social order and expectations, and start reaching out to each other and rejoining with our loved ones, including estranged families.

People have been taught to sit back and let the government find ways to fix problems, or sit back and pray that someone with a higher power will. The only one who can fix our problems is us! We must wake up every morning with a smile and thankful that we have another day to change our life, by bringing as much happiness as we can to ourselves and others. Get involved with your churches and volunteer a couple hours on your day off to helping others, like cleaning someone's house, taking them shopping, cooking a wonderful meal, and much, much more. Get involved with your community by getting people together for social gatherings like carnivals, dances, picnics, and league games like bowling, softball and volleyball. There is so much we can do for each other. Spirits are born to a family because they are drawn to their energy, and feel the parents are best suited to meet their needs. You and the Cosmos chose your parents, which is why it is so important to love and respect each other. We must concentrate on developing nurturing relationships between parents and children, and all siblings. Even estranged families will help each other when no one else will. Family is essential. Spouses felt a special bond when they first met, which lead them to marriage, but the depression (evil) in their lives places a bridge between them, making them doubt themselves, and each other. We must proclaim our love and start living the way we're supposed to!

Don't wait for the Holistic Government to make the changes. Start doing everything you can right now to change our world! Start eating healthy foods and portions, exercise using yoga form, meditate, and do fun activities with your loved ones. Protest companies that are full of corruption and are polluting our environment, and put your money into organizations that are making positive changes. Monitor the actions of people and anonymously report all corruption to news reporters and any organization making improvements to our world. Criminals, including the secret society, will try to embezzle all the money they can and hide it away, but when the new governance is elected and implemented, their money will have no power. Therefore, you must not wait for the election of the new governance, because your actions will be getting monitored on a continual basis by people who care, and you never being aware of it. There are hackers, who are employed by the government, that can infiltrate any computer system, and avoid being detected. They will be willing to compile hidden information and send it anonymously to the public. The American people are highly educated and independent, but have been very naive in believing what the mass media and government is telling them. They want so much to believe that they voted for someone they can trust, that they are willing to bury the truth by accepting all their false propaganda. Governments have been lying to us since they were first formed! When the people started doubting them, and challenging them, the government imprisoned anyone who spoke against them, like during the McCarthy Trials and Salem witch hunts. It should be considered a war crime to drop a nuclear bomb on innocent people, bomb milk factories in starving countries, or even bomb your own trade center, but the American government has, and continues to get away with it. The people need to stop being the government's puppets and guinea pigs, and take charge of their own lives and environment, because if we don't, we will surely die! If disease has not yet stricken you, it's at your doorstep, and no matter how rich one might be, these diseases will take your life also, especially viruses that have been man-made.

The greatest killers of mankind today are diseases of the limbic system, which controls the endocrine and autoimmune systems. Endocrine diseases are things like diabetes and hypothyroidism. Autoimmune diseases are high blood pressure, allergies, cancers, palsies, and many more. Very few die of injuries and associated complications, which are the only medical concerns people should have, but thousands pass on every day from starvation and limbic system diseases. Also, all psychiatric disorders are located in the limbic system. We must utilize the knowledge of the chakras and Maslow's Hierarch of Needs. The basic needs of survival and love and belonging must be met before someone can have the ability to see their true self. This cannot be done by the use of pills. Pills, which are concentrated forms of plants and dangerous chemicals, should only be used in emergencies. We need a good diet, exercise, security and happiness to heal. Only through holistic living can one be healthy, so get off the couch, eat right and have fun! The knowledge of life has been gained through centuries of people from all cultures learning what to use, when to use it and how to use it. Unfortunately, this knowledge is quickly being lost as the elders pass away, but there are several organizations that are searching earnestly for this knowledge, offering books and workshops, and they should be the ones who are consulted or elected for the Healthcare Committee. The Committee will develop all the standards for care, policies and procedures to be used in all facilities, and job descriptions for everyone, including doctors. All facilities will be uniform in their methods of treatments, documentation, and ways of educating all healthcare staff on holistic medicine. Holistic medicine will utilize every practice known to have healing results like organic herbs and food, earth, sun, water, yoga, reflexology, massage, and many more. Healthcare is the rehabilitation of the physical, mental and spiritual being of a person, which means teaching them about their disease process, treatments, and the prevention of complications and reoccurrences. Proper education is the key to success which spans across all areas. Through proper education and dedication, we can maintain a holistic life forever!

The Education Committee will focus on organized education, ranging from preschool through college and trade schooling. The Education Committee will develop the curriculum for all schools, using the most effective methods known, including patented programs. The Committee will specify all resources and equipment that are needed for each school, giving every child the opportunity to find and expand their interests and talents. All schools will be provided holistic books, art supplies, sports equipment, swimming pools, and electronic devices, and will teach every form of art like music, acting, dance, sculpture, painting and much more. Likewise, schools will teach all sports and have athletic competitions. Every student is special with a goal to meet, and will have equal opportunity in all the arts and athletics to find their interests and talents in the elementary and middle schools. Just because someone is better doesn't mean that they get more opportunities to perform. Practice makes perfect. By high school everyone should know what they like and are good at, and will focus their learning and practice in those areas. High school will be self directed in which the teachers and students will work closely together to find and develop their interests and talents, along with learning all the essentials of life. Essentials of life, which are activities of daily living, are classes like learning how to plan and cook healthy meals, exercise and meditate, have healthy and loving relationships, stay clean and organized, use time wisely, handle emergencies, and perform basic repair and maintenance on things like cars, appliances, plumbing and more. Schools will teach you how to live safely and holistically, and how to explore the world in a responsible way. Students will be expected to know information taught to them, not just remembering it for a test, and will be tested periodically, throughout their years in school. Remember, the mind has photographic memory. The students in high school will choose their classes. Not everyone needs advanced math and sciences. However, they must attend classes on, activities of daily living, physical science, reading and writing, and areas of interest because these are the things that will teach us how to live the life that's best for us. All education will begin with the basics, and every year will build on that information, reaching higher levels of understanding. Children's minds are like great sponges, and are capable of retaining vast amounts of knowledge, if introduced holistically, connecting everything to life. Even telepathy, telekinesis and others can, and will be, learned.

The Ecology Committee will focus on identifying and implementing the most effective, efficient and quickest ways to cleanse the air, earth and water. They will develop programs for recycling, and supply all the people and every business with recycling containers and methods for proper elimination, even garbage can be recycled for compost. Anyone not following the rules will be committing a crime and be dealt with accordingly. Landfills will be cleansed. The natural flow of all water will be restored by strategically and gradually opening up all damned areas, replenishing dried up streams, and providing life to areas that had been destroyed. Lakes and streams should be the size they were intended to be, not what the rich says they should be. Besides, there are plenty of naturally occurring lakes to play on, but must be enjoyed holistically, not allowing any pollutants to enter the water. If you are afraid of flooding, which still occurs with reservoirs, don't build so close to waterfronts, or build higher up with break walls. People have no right to change the natural flow of water, only Gaia does. Water belongs to all, therefore all land within a specified distance from any free flowing water, like rivers and creeks that return to the rivers, and lakes fed by rivers, will be considered public. You can still have property that leads up to the water, but all fences will be a specific distance away, and not allowed to cross over any flowing stream. However, if you have property where people can stop to camp, you have the right to obtain their identity and license number, and report all damages, including trash left behind. Also, the property owners will have priority over the use of the area, if they are currently planning on using it. You may not prevent others for the use of naturally occurring water, because no one can own the water, but you can provide camp sites, water parks and more. Everyone, no matter who you are, deserves the opportunities to play in water, and enjoy all the beautiful creations that Gaia has provided. In reality, Gaia would rather have a poor, loving and happy person enjoy her creations, instead of someone who is greedy, and puts up walls and fences around it, forcing people to stay out.

All state parks and museums will be maintained by the Community Centers, providing everyone with recreation. No spiritual landmarks, like chakras and magnificent creations of Gaia, will be designated as private land by anyone, because Gaia wants everyone to enjoy all of her beautifully, magnificent creations. Parks must have no barriers except the outside fence, and secured areas, so that the animals and people can move about freely. The parks will be cleansed of any debris on a continuous basis. However, people who want to go off trail, without guides, or go floating down rivers, must have a license to do so. In order to get a nature's license, which includes fishing, hunting, camping, boating and more, you must pass a test on the laws of the land, designed by the Ecology Committee. People without a license will be restricted to secured areas. Clean water is more valuable than all the gold in the world, therefore no dumping of any kind will be allowed. All areas of Gaia will be cleansed of radioactive and chemical waste. If the waste can't be disposed of in safe ways, then that product will be banned along with the use of all fossil fuels, nuclear reactors, plastics, fluoride, and any other toxic substance. There are holistic ways to keep your teeth clean and healthy. Deep mining must be stopped! Everything you could possibly need is found on the surface. Gaia has provided us with many safe and useful resources for building and technology, and all the energy we could ever need with renewable resources that are very inexpensive to harness and distribute to the entire world! There are already many programs available that provide safe and clean energy, and if the money being spent on wars was spent on these programs, the damages to Gaia could be reversed quickly. Once the health of Gaia has been restored, many species thought to be extinct, will start to live again.

The Agriculture Committee will identify the healthiest foods and herbs to restore health and balance to people's lives. They will use only natural methods for pest control and to establish and maintain healthy soils. All foods will be grown using the sun and rain water. Scientists believe that they can genetically improve foods but they are so very wrong. Only our Mother Earth can give birth to foods and herbs. The synthetic hormones and chemicals being used, alter vegetation and are poisonous to people and animals. The bodies of people and animals have become so polluted that the immune system identifies them as foreign, and tries to destroy them as seen in some cancers, arthritis, palsies and other autoimmune diseases. People have blamed the sun for skin cancer, but it's the toxins in their bodies that cause the disease. The sun, air, water and earth are all healing to the body when used correctly, by killing harmful bacteria and pulling toxins out of the body. However, since our sun is radioactive, exposure must be limited, but only until our original magnetic suns can be reborn. Once the body is cleansed, good vitamins, minerals, fats and proteins can replenish the body with healthy cells. Cleansing the body also means cleansing the mind. Mental stress has direct effects on the immune system and hormonal levels because it is the mind that controls them. The greatest stress is internal conflict. Internal conflict is as simple as procrastination, to dissociative disorders like schizophrenia and DIDS. This develops when a person has been so traumatized that they actually separate themselves into different personalities or withdraw into an isolated world, both trying to protect their psyche from the evil around them. Some abuse is so severe that the child withdraws, but other forms of abuse are done in ways where the child learns to accept it as part of life. They've been taught that physical punishment is for the good of the child, and to enjoy being raped even if it hurts. However, since the psyche knows that they are special and sacred, they build emotional walls around them, keeping them isolated and non-trusting. They eventually become abusers mainly to themselves, and surround themselves with others who are also abusive. A large part of the world suffers from some level of this disorder, and are often seen as chronic liars because their psyche can't accept the bad that they are doing, so they block it out. People have also learned that they can deny their actions or change the truth of the events that occurred, with false memories. This disorder is very difficult to correct because the wall people build around the psyche is very strong and keep them in the dark. It's hard to help someone when they don't even know there is a problem, but can be done with proper rehabilitation. This mental stress can be relieved once a person realizes that the past is simply an experience in life that no longer has to control their present life. At any given moment, a person can realize the truly special person they are and let go of all the negative feelings of guilt and hate and open their heart and soul. Hormonal imbalances occur during fetal development, so every newborn will be tested, and any imbalance corrected. Physical and mental stress is also caused by unhealthy diets and lack of activity, and it's the lack of proper nutrition that causes laziness and procrastination.

The Agricultural Committee and Healthcare Committee will work closely in developing farms with foods and herbs that are best for curing diseases and autoimmune disorders, and giving the people lots of energy to get motivated and make changes. The Committee will also build enormous greenhouse like structures over all wastelands and start new growth of resonant ecosystems. Everyone interested in farming will be given all the assistance and resources needed because farming will be a high priority. Also restaurants will offer healthy foods in appropriate portions and stores will have prepackaged healthy meals. Grains will not be bleached or robbed of their nutrition in any way. Foods can be processed without losing their nutritional value and life force, and can appeal to the tastes of everyone. The human body was designed to ingest fruits, vegetables, grains and fish, but due to times of famine, which was a result of greed, people were forced to eat bloody meats and flour products. Every culture has specific foods and herbs that can nurture their bodies and cure all aliments. Genealogy plays an important role in the foods and herbs that are right for us, which is why soul testing will be done on everyone to find the specific needs of each person. People have got to get back to the basics and start eating healthy and good tasting foods, and reestablish our roots and spiritual bonds.

The Law Enforcement Committee will develop holistic job descriptions for all military personnel with specific missions for each company, and all law enforcement, from local police to FBI and CIA. They will set the standards for receiving reports of all crimes and protecting the informant's identity under the Amnesty Clause. The informant's however, will be judged if the charges are found to be false or under malice. The Healthcare Committee will be involved in developing programs to convert prisons into secured rehabilitation centers bringing holistic care to all convicts. All criminals, and their families will receive holistic rehabilitation, and be assigned a social service case manager, who will place them into the community safely and holistically, creating a holistic life for them. The Committee will design ways to identify abuse in the homes, schools, and places of employment, or by referrals like emergency rooms. The questions will be specifically designed to identify different types of mental illnesses, abuse and neglect in the homes and any area of corruption. The questions will detect when someone is deliberately answering them falsely, in which the person will receive a personal interview. The questions will also give everyone the opportunity to admit all their crimes and illegal interactions. It is at this time when people can ask for help and amend their wrongdoings. Anyone who fails to report themselves at this time, and later found guilty of a crime or abuse, will be required to be placed in a rehabilitation center until success is achieved. The severity of the crime and the mental stability of the person will determine the level of rehabilitation. <u>All</u> armament will be converted to a sedating gas or liquid, or sonic pulsations that limit a person's mobility long enough to be apprehended. No one will be harmed, and everyone will be treated with respect. Those who are out of control will be placed in a quiet, nurturing place. People will become friends with each other and with animals as Gaia restores the balance of nature, bringing harmony to us all. The law enforcement will take all criminals to rehabilitation centers or camps for large groups of people, like militias who refuse to accept this holistic way of living. Special forces will infiltrate all areas of corruption, bringing down those who resist and helping those who cooperate. The only military action will be for protection. No country, or secret society, will be allowed to enter another country, or domain, and forcible take from them!

The Social Service Committee will ensure the proper implementation of all rehabilitation programs in the homes. Monitors will be placed in identified abusive homes and places of employment, including churches. People will bc monitored for inappropriate behavior and taught how to correct it. They will also be taught how to plan their day so that they can complete all the activities of daily living. These activities include personal hygiene, preparing and eating three healthy meals with snacks in between, cleaning up afterwards, eight hours of work or school, eight to nine hours of healthy sleep, and at least two hours for fun and relaxation. All places of employment will offer every full time employee thirty minutes to exercise, either before or after work, and supply them a place to do so. This can be a room added on or converted, or a spa membership. The healthcare policies will also incorporate exercise. Programs will provide the people with all the physical and emotional assistance needed to achieve a holistic life. Mothers feeling overwhelmed and deciding to place their child up for adoption will receive special attention. Spirits choose, with the help of the Cosmos, when to be reborn and to whom. The time of one's birth depends on their vibration, and family depends on their lineage. Becoming a parent is truly a blessing and should be treated as such. Families will have only one person working so one parent can stay home at all times teaching and nurturing their children. It is very important for the mother to stay home until the child reaches age four, then the father can choose to stay home. This is so the child can receive breast feeding, which is very important for their physical and emotional development, and so they can develop strong and healthy chakras, which can be achieved with consistent nurturing. Everything will be done to keep families together, but when divorce does happen, the children will be placed with the stable parent, or foster home if needed, and given holistic care. However, the couples will receive holistic rehabilitation together, and be shown how their love has connected them to the Divine, and hopefully will see the truly beautiful person their spouse is by remembering that Divine spark that first attracted them. The Social Service Committee will be the liaison between family members and their Community Center, ensuring that everyone receive holistic rehabilitation. Rehabilitation also means public education which can be obtained quickly and effectively through media and telecommunications.

The Media and Telecommunication Committee will provide all access channels with informational programs according to age, stage of development, and interests, entertaining sit-coms and movies, true historical and scientific events, personal accounts of adventures, games, mysteries, and loving transmissions form Gaia and ascending channels. However, there will be set hours of no programming, including all expanded channels, to help encourage people to get off the couch and live life. The Committee will set specific restrictions on internet use. There will be limited adult content on the internet, and will be used only in exchange of information, playing appropriate games, obtaining items, and chatting responsibly with other people. Adult chat rooms will be available but accessed only with registered codes, and heavily monitored for illegal content like child, animal, or violent pornography. Visual contact will be allowed, with children also, but monitored for inappropriate behavior and language. All cd's will be marked either as a personal recording, or a professional recording. This will prevent pirating. The internet is an amazing tool but must be used holistically. All movies, shows, commercials, radio announcements, and music will be rated based on level of destruction and adult content, implied or explicit. Adults will still be allowed to obtain adult rated material but only at state stores in adult communities, where such content is monitored. State stores and adult communities will be the only places to obtain controlled items. Controlled items are identified as anything that can cause harm to the physical, mental and spiritual well being of a person. These items include, but not limited to, cigarettes, alcohol, cocaine, marijuana, and adult media and materials. The amount of items will be placed on national records and anyone found exceeding the approved levels of consumption, or found with these items unsecured in homes where children reside or visit, or in public places, will be detained and evaluated for rehabilitation. Most of these drugs were designed to control the minds of others by altering or enhancing their original state. Some, when used correctly, under structure and guidance, can lighten the psyche and open doors to the soul that have been closed. There are also medicinal uses with some drugs like mescaline for schizophrenia, and marijuana for intractable nausea and glaucoma, but cigarettes and alcohol are some of the most addictive and destructive drugs, and as people become rehabilitated, will be banned. Media has the power to educate people through inspirational and informative programs, and can facilitate positive feelings with adventurous, mysterious, heart-warming, comical and dramatic programs and movies. When radio and television were first introduced, people were at war with misery all around them. It provided the people a means of forgetting about the war for a little while by having some entertainment. When the governments saw the impact television had on people, they started using it to influence the thoughts and actions of people through false propaganda. They emphasized the negativity in the world in a parody fashion which calloused people from the death and destruction around them. They showed families and neighbors harming each other which encouraged people to start doubting their neighbors and blaming others for their problems. The bonds between families and neighbors were broken. The government then split up the families even more, by offering people high paying jobs to relocate, and then, when the government set up economic depressions, life became a struggle for most. News was one sided, emphasizing the evil in the world, and showing violence in the streets which scared people into staying in their homes, and not trusting others. People became introverts and addicted to television, providing the people with a false sense of security, pseudo friends and propaganda about the happenings in the world. They've got people looking at evil like it's only some monster on television, but evil is a part of nearly everyone's lives on a daily basis, and will continue to rob us of our lives. All telecommunications and media must be used responsibly, therefore lies, misleading news programs, and promotion of evil, will not be tolerated. We must emphasize the good things and deeds in the world!

The Land Development Committee will identify all the areas of Gaia being harmed, or could be harmed by building on them, or by being stripped of natural resources. They will set the standards for the development of all buildings, bridges, roads and others. The construction of roads will be done quickly, using the most effective methods known, and will not impair the normal flow of traffic. Roads and highways will be designed to facilitate even movement of traffic by timing the lights accordingly, and signs like yield and merge, will mean every other vehicle, starting with the one who reaches there first. No one should have to sit and wait for others, or sit at long traffic lights. This just encourages road rage. All busy intersections will have a light or four way stop. All roadways will have safe bicycle lanes. Structures that are placing too much stress in an area will be moved or destroyed and all areas restored, including swamp lands, and especially rain forests. Every area of development will have a specific percentage of the land used for parks and recreation, and all businesses will have areas for trees and flowers. There will also be a specified amount of land anyone can claim, including the amount of waterfront property, based on if it is for personal use or a business, allowing more for ranches, farms, parks and natural preserves. All land that is not claimed by someone will belong to the Community Center in which the land is governed, and given to others who choose to live in that Community. The Committee will also work closely with the Ecology Committee in designing the most effective sewer systems for waste elimination and rain run-off, which must be separated. Rain water will be used for gardens, and in cleaners and other similar products. Aquifers and springs will be used for drinking water, and all recycled waste waters will be used for waste removal, and stored for the use of emergencies. All homes and businesses will have three inlet pipes and two outlet pipes. One inlet pipe will carry recycled water for waste removal, another with only naturally purified water for consumption, and rain run-off for lawn and garden. One outlet pipe will carry waste water and the other rain run-off, which will lead to different sewer systems. The salt and impurities in the ocean will be filtered and the water used to put out fires and hydrate dried up lands. The Committee will implement programs that will supply everyone who has a yard with trees, flowers, orchards and holistic gardens. The roadsides will be covered with wild flowers and herbs native to that area. Tribal people, who still live by the laws of the land, will receive great rewards for helping to replenish the land and teach others how to. They will also be given great open areas, including certain areas of state parks, in which they can reside without interference and hopefully remember ancestral traditions, that have been nearly lost.

The Energy Committee will work closely with the Ecology Committee in developing ways to convert all vehicles and machinery into safe and productive ones, using only clean energy, and programs that will provide everyone with homes and businesses that are powered with the love of magnetic energy. The solar system supplies us with endless energy from solar, wind, and lightning in storms, which can all be harnessed and stored easily, providing everyone with temporary safe and healthy energy. Vehicles and machines, of all types, will be traded in for electric ones of equal value, that is until everything can be converted to magnetic energy. Nuclear contamination threatens the very existence of Gaia and must be dealt with immediately and safely! This is of top priority and every effort must be made to convert as quickly as possible. Everyone deserves to be supplied with an endless and holistic form of energy, but must be responsible and comply with all regulations.

The Peer Review Committee will design programs to be implemented in all places of business and rehabilitation. This is a major task and very important. Monitoring the actions of everyone is a very sensitive issue and must be done in a very respectful and holistic way. Peers are coworkers and neighbors, and they are the ones who will evaluate the public for misconduct. All businesses and communities will have their own Peer Review Committee, comprised of people elected by the employees of a business, neighbors in a community, or members of an Executive Cabinet. They will evaluate everyone reported and recommend appropriate forms of rehabilitation or probation monitoring. The findings will be sent to the Community Center's law enforcement, where it will be placed on national records, and the proper rehabilitation provided. The idea is not to punish and then forget, but to help everyone achieve a holistic life! You may think that it will cost too much to design and supply the people with these programs. The truth is, if we took the money people pay right now for taxes and fees, everyone could be given all the wonderful things in life, like nice homes, clothes, recreation, and travels. This nice life was never meant for just the rich. Gaia provides everything people need, which belongs to everyone, and everyone has a specific talent and knowledge that will benefit the Whole. Everyone is valuable and the Holistic Governance would be able to discover everyone's interests and talents. The Community Centers will unite people by holding social affairs, like carnivals, picnics, sports and more. They will provide everyone with enough resources to enjoy life to the fullest. What has been presented here in this book, is just the basics to get us started. We have all the knowledge and resources needed to achieve this wonderful way of life, but we must stop evil from controlling us, and achieving world domination. The "New World Order" will be freedom and health for everyone! It's all up to us. We must get involved and stop believing what the governments, and many religions, are telling us, and demand the implementation of the Holistic Governance! All we need to do is elect holistic people this fall for our new way of life!!

There are great leaders all over the world with great knowledge and insight that are ready to help us. This has been reflected in art like the song Imagine, where you realize there is no religion only spiritualism, the movie

Powder, where one becomes connected to the Cosmos, and the movie Contact, that shows how we live on different planes within the same Cosmos, and have the ability to reach higher levels of existence. The only way we can reach our center being is by living a healthy, loving and happy life, and by finding our center soul through complete self awareness and actualization. There is currently a huge movement of people searching for religion and spiritual enlightenment as never seen before, and that's because the spirit in people are aware that the time is drawing near for the end of this world. Although religions are separate with different beliefs, most have the essential things in common, the belief that there is only one supreme being, which of course is themselves, and that one must live life in a peaceful and loving way to reach liberation or heaven. Spiritual truth has been lost through peoples mislead interpretations of spiritual teachings, resulting in man's laws, not the Divine. Holism is the good in all religions, practices meditation, and provides unconditional love, and enlightenment. Holism is simply to live your life the way your soul tells you to, which can only be heard through an open and calm mind. Eat healthy, exercise, work hard at what you do best, have lots of fun and treat everyone with love and respect. If you treat yourself and your environment with unconditional love, then you will make all the right decisions for your life, and will find your special calling, which will help bring balance to the Whole and your ascension to the next higher level. People believe that God will forgive them for all their sins if they confess, but they themselves are God. Therefore, forgiveness can only come from within yourself.

The only way people can forgive themselves is by admitting their wrongdoings to themselves and the ones they've harmed, ask for forgiveness from those they've harmed, and change their lives into loving ones. Though people believe in a religion that stands for love and truth, there is still turmoil. People who believe in love and freedom wish to live their lives peacefully, allowing others, who are driven by greed and hate, to take control over their environment. No matter how much one prays and meditates, and follows their gospel, when people around them are causing them and their loved ones harm, that harmony is disrupted. You need an environment that is calm, orderly and nurturing. The people of the world must come together now and decide jointly that they want a healthy and happy world to live in. It is our right to have clean water and air, friendly neighborhoods, recreation for everyone, and a governance that ensures the safety and betterment of all people.

Many great spirits have taught repeatedly that we are all connected to each other and the only way to reach God is to love with all your heart, soul and mind, and to live life to the fullest. Some believe this means that the goal in life is to transcend physical desires and abide with God in eternal peace, but God is life and life is growth, which can only be achieved through continuous experiences and memories. This physical world was created by the love of all created, allowing us to experience the extreme joys of physical manifestation like, feeling a loving touch, smelling sweet flowers, tasting wonderful foods, seeing the depth in colors and a loving smile, and hearing the most beautiful music of all, the laughter of all life, which includes coos from babies, purrs from loving cats, and happy barks from loyal dogs. The true goal for everyone is to find true love, live in harmony and ascend to a state of pure ecstasy. It is meaningless if only a few reach enlightenment when the rest remain in darkness. If one does reach liberation, finding their place with God/ Brahma, they will also suffer and mourn the loss of all the lost and tortured souls. Jesus did not die on the cross to forgive our sins but to show how God, the Divine, suffers and mourns for all the lost souls, and to teach that if we live our lives as he instructed, to love unconditionally as God loves, we will reach higher levels of existence, with much more to experience, as seen through his resurrection. All these great ancient spiritualists have a deep understanding of the Divine and how weak the Cosmos has become by the evil dominating this world, and knows that only a strong life force can stop the evil's influence and control. A life force is any thought or action that is loving, helpful and nurturing. That's why they all taught that the most important thing to do was to love yourself, and everything around you with all your heart, soul and mind, and treat everyone as if they were God, which in fact they are.

People have had great difficulty understanding the truth of their religion. People want to believe that God is outside of them, who can forgive them and change their lives to the way they want them to be. Unfortunately, people also believe that they are superior to others, which separates them from the Cosmos, and convinces them that they are separate from animals, animals separate from insects,

insects from plants, and plants from water and soil, but they are all wrong. Even the King James Bible states that man came from dust. People also want to believe that they could live outside of Earth, in other galaxies. This is just a dream, in hopes that someday they can escape their world of destruction. Non indigenous people can only return to their original place of birth through the star gates which requires the knowledge and assistance of Gaia. We are all connected to the Cosmos, with the purpose to love and grow, and by living life holistically we can return HOME. Life is a continuous journey where one grows by learning and experiencing, and ascending or descending to different levels of existence. Our current life is a crossroad giving us opportunities to become one with the Cosmos. Depending on how you lead your life, you may ascend to a higher state of awareness, descend to a lower state of darkness, or remain in the confused and stagnant state that most of us have confined ourselves to. Gaia provides the knowledge and resources needed to ascend to higher levels of non-physical worlds, but without Gaia we will no longer have that opportunity and will remain in a state of confusion and darkness for all eternity. Everyone has experienced the Divine to some degree, from deja vues, ghost encounters, and enlightenment to visions. We all know deep down that there are always mysterious forces around, even the scientists and atheists. This is the energy of our spiritual essence and the energy from Gaia's chakras which are directly connected to the chakras in our bodies. Sometimes, if it is important enough to help balance the energy in the Cosmos, spirits in other planes of existence can send their energy to you by the way of miracles. Good and bad luck are simply the energy one draws towards themselves through attraction. If you have loving and creative thoughts and feelings, you will draw opportunities and miracles to you, but if you are depressed and angry, bad things will continue to happen to you. If your life force is focused and loving, you can send this Divine energy to others with magnificent effects, bringing them good fortune and love. This is what Gaia is doing for us. She is releasing all her energy to us so she can wake us up and show us the way to salvation, but if we remain in the dark and refuse her love, we will stop her ascension, which is why we must act fast. Gaia is becoming critically unstable through millenniums of pollution, stripping of natural resources, and the use of deadly carbon based and nuclear energy. All of this evil energy is preventing the chakras from absorbing healthy energy and releasing used energy, which will cause Gaia to fragment and no one, even in space, will survive!

All great spiritual leaders taught how to love and find the truth in all things, not that giving money to a church will give you a place in God's Kingdom. In fact, they all refused monetary offerings and lived simple lives. The clergy of any church should live a simple life and use the donations wisely, by providing their congregation and community with needed things like food, housing, clothing, jobs and more. Churches should be places that unite neighborhoods by offering love and acceptance, not by being televised to another country. These huge ministries that bring in millions every week should have corrected the problems in most poor areas. They say that they have started outreach programs worldwide yet people in their own town live in broken down homes and struggle every day to feed and clothe their families. Entire areas like in the Appalachians and Indian reservations are severely poor with rampant disease and abuse, yet no one offers to help them. It's easy to say you're helping others when people can't follow up and confirm it, or the people you're so-called helping, don't believe in your religion. Besides, people shouldn't be sitting in their homes watching church services, they should be attending church with their families and friends, and people who can't attend, should be given a video of the service by their clergy and prayer groups, allowing them to also participate. Listen. The Divine is not asking for money, but for your love. Offering your time and services to helping others means much more than money, but if you see a church who is actually cleaning up neighborhoods, taking food to the poor, offering to clean homes and giving transportation to the elderly and disabled, then please send donations to help continue this glorious work. Any church that demands an offering and claims that only through a monetary offering can you find grace with God, are lying to you! A clergy that opens a church in a poor, high crime area, offering friendship and love to the people who had lost hope, is doing more for the Cosmos than all the global ministries. However, some of these ministries teach people how to deal with daily life in a real and spiritual way, but they must offer their books and workshops free to people who can't afford them, start helping people in their communities and own country, and start living a simple life, not a glamorous one. The clergy needs to bring friendship, recreation, and truth to their congregations. Remember, God is not an outside entity looking down and judging us. It is the life force inside all of us that connects us to everyone and every living thing, and what we feel in our hearts, is what we live in our souls, and we bring that energy to the Whole.

Countries can have their cultural and religious differences yet be the same in living holistic lives. True holistic living is the purest form of thought and emotions that are on the path to becoming one with ourselves. It is only obtained when an entity completely cleanses their body, mind, and soul, and learns through intense focus and dedication, how to use all of their mind and control their emotions. Life is a constant state of being with no death, only transformations, which is determined by your own level of self awareness and actualization. If you are harmful to animals, you may be reborn as an animal to learn the value of their life and feelings. If you are a murderer or rapist may be reborn as a victim. If you are lost, you may wander the Cosmos indefinitely as an angry ghost, until you find your path which can only be found by facing your true self, and determining which path will help you grow. If, at the time of your passing, you're living a healthy and loving life, you will see the truly special person you are, and be able to decide what is best for you. You may also find other spirits that you have formed strong bonds with, that is as long as they are open enough to sense you. It is possible that your child is a great grandparent, or spiritual leader, depending on their life force. The more chakras that are cleansed and functioning properly, the higher the level of existence one can ascend. The purpose of life is to learn and grow, and always be filled with love, and the way to do this is to have a healthy and nurturing environment. Everyone deserves a happy and healthy life. It makes no difference if you are a criminal or a holy person. Everyone has the power within to change their thoughts and emotions into positive ones. The right way to treat people is to believe that everyone is of equal value. Men and women can't own anyone but themselves. Therefore they can't do whatever they want to their children and spouses, they must respect their feelings. Everyone who asks for respect deserves respect, but the only way to ask for respect is by respecting yourself and others. When a person acts in a negative way, they are showing disrespect for themselves. One must live by the way of the Divine before they can respect themselves, and be respected by others. To live holistically, is to treat everyone and everything with loving care. Men have been taught that they are not supposed to be loving and show affection, as it shows weakness, but they are so wrong. Everyone is born to love and be loved. A child will choose a loving touch over food. Everyone is guided by their emotions. We live to love and love to live, and every life we live, gives us opportunities to open the doors to our souls and find oneness with ourselves. This life we're living is simply an experience in our total life, which never ends, unless evil devours it. People are truly part of the Cosmos and have the ability to gain strength and wisdom from the energies that are constantly surrounding us, but you must be spiritually centered and open to the wonders of the universe.

No one can tell you what the Divine has in store for you. Only you have that answer and the only way to hear what your soul is telling you, is to believe in yourself and learn how to quiet your mind through prayer and meditation. Love is every great idea that comes to you. Your soul knows everything that is happening in the Cosmos and knows where you need to be, who you need to talk to, and what you need to do that will answer your questions and bring you what you desire and need. Most importantly, never procrastinate! When your soul speaks, listen to what it has to say and act right then, or you may lose your opportunity. Your soul only speaks what is right. All negative thoughts come from your own insecurities which were developed by separating yourself from your center being. Everyone's talents and desires are different which brings balance to the Cosmos. Not everyone wants to be rich. Many just want to live a simple, peaceful and loving life while others want to lead, invent or help others. Churches can be a wonderful place to learn this if they become what they were meant to be. A designated place where people can join together in fellowship and enlightened ones can teach others how to live holistically. However, just because someone joins the ministry, doesn't mean that they are enlightened. Beware of evil in disguise because it can deceive and confuse you. If it doesn't feel right, then it's not and you need to move on. Fellowship is the joy of opening ourselves up to others so that we may feel and share their energies. However, people must feel safe in doing so. We need places where we have a sense of belongingness, and feel safe in sharing ourselves with the people there.

Not only are people different physically, but spiritually also. Everyone is drawn to different things and beliefs such as favorite art, music, foods and fragrance, but also to different religions and practices. Some religions like that of American Indians and Wicca, teach to worship Gaia and all her elements, others like Buddhism and Hinduism teach to worship the self and soul, and others like Christianity, Judaism and Islam teach to worship the teachings given by their spiritual leader. They all have truth but separated will never reach the Divine. Only through Holism can the centre be reached. Holism encompasses the good in all religions and exposes all the lies and corruption. Holism is the union of the body, and the spirit of the self, guided by the energies of the Cosmos, and the Holy Spirit, or chakras, that connects us all. The father-Cosmos, the mother-Earth, and the child-You. All religions that condone harming others, be it person, animal or plant, must be banned. When plants are sacrificed for the good of people, the people need to praise and thank them for giving their life force, which is why you need to pray at all meals and at the time of planting and harvest and also when drinking water. All places of worship are sacred, which brings people together to share and learn in peace and harmony. They should be places where the congregation is provided with truth and love, and allowed to perform their sacred rituals, and share their experiences with others, without being judged or ridiculed. It should also be a time to enjoy healthy foods, music, dance and laughter.

When the Gnostics met for church, they drew lots to see what role they would assume for the day. One was designated as priest which led the gatherings, and the bishop who offered sacrament. Some would read from the scriptures, while others would provide spiritual instructions as prophets. The rest of the congregation would sing and dance. They believed that since the Divine directs everything, the way the lots fell expressed the divine choice because the energies of the Cosmos knew what needed to be said and done, that would benefit the Whole. Their goal was to achieve Awen, balance. Just because you have been trained to be a priest or minister, doesn't mean that you are an expert. The poor humble man in your congregation could be much closer to the Divine, and more qualified at giving spiritual guidance than the priest. Places of worship should supply the people with picnics or carnivals full of fun and exploration, which everyone needs, because no matter how old you are, there is a child inside of you eager to get out and have fun. This does not include being served alcohol, which is one of "Man's" evil creations. Spoiled grains and fruit are poisonous and should not be ingested. The practice of Christian's Holy Communion, should symbolize their devotion by drinking purified water and eating grains, fruits and vegetables.

Everyone needs a place where they won't be judged and where others won't try to control them. The only one who can judge you is you, because only you can answer the question that needs to be answered. Am I living the life I need in order to achieve self actualization and full potential? People will always make impressions of others based on the way they act, but respectful people will never treat them bad because of those impressions. They will try to help them, or just avoid them. The only judging in a holistic world is by yourself, or by people trying to determine the truth of events, and the guilt or innocence of the parties involved. People aren't born wanting to be bad, they've learned to be that way because of the way others have treated them. When children are abused and neglected, they learn to be abusive and neglectful, especially to themselves.

Everyone has the innate desire to do good things and be liked by others. We are driven by our need for love and acceptance. However, when you have been taught to be ashamed of yourself, and blame yourself for all the harm that has come to you, you learn to hate or fear yourself and the world around you. People go to their grave, actual rebirth, believing that they are bad or evil and don't deserve anything good. They live in the hell they created, or wander aimlessly. They can't find their way because they don't believe they are special, and their past of fear, greed, or hate is so strong, that they can't see that there is a better life for them. However, a strong life force like Gaia's can reach us, if we let her, and show us how to climb out of this pit of darkness. The collective force of evil is so great that everyone's lives are influenced by it, and most are actually infected by it. Infected with an incredibly devastating disease, Silent Depression, just like in the song The Sound of Silence, and it goes with you when you pass on. All you have are your memories and emotions, and if they are infected with this horrible disease of separation and misalignment, you can never ascend. We must purge ourselves and Gaia's chakras of evil, and fill our world, and the Cosmos with a strong life force. If the people started getting healthy and feeling good about themselves, the collective forces would change to a healthy energy, and start effecting people in a Holistic way through miracles and good luck. Good things would happen that would guide people to their path of freedom and happiness!

All we have to do is start thinking new thoughts, but this is no simple task. To create new thoughts, one must be vibrating at their perfect spiritual vibration, regardless if their form is physical or non physical. We all choose how to express our energy in any form based on our level of self awareness and how we see ourselves. Do we see ourselves as the perfect life forms or by the opinions of a descended humanity? If we are not seeing ourselves as perfect creations, capable of creating a perfect life for ourselves, then we are not resonating at our spiritual vibration. In order to become aware of our perfect inner self, we must eliminate all thoughts of imperfection, and remember all the magnificent thoughts that we've forgotten. Only then can we break past this barrier that keeps us in the past, and prevents us from creating a future. Evil has us believing that the reality of who we are is science fiction, and that anyone showing signs of mental powers are freaks and need to be subdued. People are fearful of ghost encounters because they would have to admit that there are unseen forces that they have no control over, which possess the power to influence their lives. The evil in our world wants the wealthy to believe that others don't deserve to have what they have and the poor to crave what they don't have. Even in villages where there are no possessions but an abundance of peace and joy, the wealthy creates turmoil in attempts to destroy their harmony and peaceful existence. Evil wants us to forget and descend into total darkness, but the Divine wants us, and needs us, to bring love, life and laughter to ourselves and each other!

As previously mentioned, there are people all over the world, in all different cultures and religions, who are uncovering the truth of all our ancestors history, communicating with every kingdom of nature, and returning their physical form back into a young and vibrant state. They are not publically known because the evil in the world keeps the average citizen unaware of the good that is happening all around the world. Evil is concentrated in organizations that have been taught that they are the superiors of the human race and that it is their responsibility to achieve and maintain dominion over humanity, even to the point of sacrificing their own lives. These lost souls who have been completely dominated by evil, want to keep the truth of our ancestries a secret, because they fear if we decipher this recorded spiritual information, we will have the ability to take back our own powers, causing them to lose all theirs. However, true power only comes from within, so everyone who chooses, can reawaken their own mental powers, including all the people who have pledged themselves to evil. They will no longer need the energy from others in attempts to dream-weave a dance of life because they'll be able to reclaim their own lost powers, and remember how to dream weave their own dance of life. Remember, mental powers only come from loving thoughts and memories, and everyone who follows their true dream, their destiny, will become the heroes of all life. Deep down everyone wants to be a hero and save the world, because only through saving the world, can we save ourselves. This is the time for our Resurrection! We need each other and I need You. I need you to get this book to as many people as you can and demand that your government implement the Divine Holistic Governance!! It's short and wouldn't take much to copy it and share it. Get it translated into every language and send it out, so everyone around the world can receive it, understand it, and live it. Please, for the sake of us all, take heed, take action, and forgive all our mistakes through your love!!!

The Cosmos' photonic belt is trying to pull us back into alignment, bringing true North back into alignment with magnetic North, which will create all the horrific storms, quakes and meteor showers, as predicted in books and movies, if we don't succeed in restoring a strong life force in Gaia's chakras. These devastating meteor showers people fear won't be Cosmic matter, as the Cosmos only wants to nurture and protect Gaia. The meteors will be all the space stations, satellites and other militaristic and surveillance debris that has been placed in Gaia's atmosphere. When the poles shift, the electromagnetic force in Gaia's aura will change and everything in the atmosphere will fall toward Gaia, crashing into cities and towns all around the globe. There will be a global wide blackout, including all electronic devices, if we don't convert to magnetic energy. No one will know where to go. Horrific ice storms will hit within seconds. Dormant volcanoes will erupt, covering surrounding cities. If we don't die from the impact and fallout of nuclear explosions, or the impact of falling spatial debris, horrific storms, tidal waves, quakes and volcanoes, we will meet our demise through spontaneous combustion. So even if you are a top national politician, or the richest person in the world, and you're hidden away deep in the Earth or on a space station, you will not be spared! However, if we are strong enough to admit the truth and start changing our lives into holistic ones, we can start removing all debris in Gaia's space, neutralize all toxins on and in Gaia, and more importantly, realign all Gaia's chakras with her centre by bringing a strong life force to her chakras. Singing, dancing a making love at the physical location of Gaia's chakras has a strong loving impact, but the greatest impact is having everyone healthy, happy and in love!!!

We could have the whole world healed within one year simply by implementing the Holistic Governance.

By sending everyone, along with their loved ones, to a holistic rehabilitation health camp they would receive all the treatments, nutrients and knowledge needed restore their bodies to the original crystalline forms they once were, receive a piece of land, as determined by Gaia, that resonates with them, complete with housing and all the furnishings that was picked out by them, when they looked through catalogs and found everything they dreamed of. Yes! Everyone can have their dream life very easily. As the experts teach people, many of the people will become teachers and teach others, and quickly we reach can reach everyone, bringing the dream to all. If today, the leaders of the world would meet together and realize that it is they who has the ability to be the saviors of all humanity, and everything in both universes, tomorrow we can begin the process by finding all the true experts in each major field, like healthcare, agriculture, ecology, economics and more, by having them place taped interviews of themselves and placing them on the internet for viewing. We elect the ones that have the best solutions to all the problems, and the governments then give them all the resources needed to form their committees and design all the programs, job descriptions, and policies and procedures to be implemented in every area of life. They will also be looking at the records of every single person, categorizing them based on health and mental needs. Those near death will be the first to receive this life changing event, followed with the poor and incarcerated. With full cooperation from the governments leaders, it should only take a few months for the cabinets to design this magnificent foundation of the

Holistic Governance. Once complete, everyone will be evaluated, treated, and given a new Holistic life, in a way that will not disrupt their lives, or the functioning of the environment. The energy of the Cosmos' photonic belt will increase our vibrations making our physical bodies look more translucent and colorful, but only if we are ready for it. If we wait for the devastation to occur because we simply choose not to believe that it is going to happen, no matter how much you repent or finally accept the truth, we will be destroyed, and eventually everyone else who is part of our Creator, including Jesus, Mohammad, and Buddha, will descend into the darkness we've all been trapped in, and Our **Creator** will eventually **die** from **Alzheimer's! WE ARE THE CONSCIOUSNESS OF OUR CREATOR. IT IS UP TO US! IT IS OUR DECISION TO LIVE OR NOT TO LIVE!! THE CREATOR IS DEPENDING ON US!!!**

Everything written in this book is based on my opinions which I believe are divinely inspired, and the absolute truth. I know I repeated things but that is to emphasize their importance. I made reference to the phrase, "numbered 144000", simply as being the perfect number, because I have no mathematical evidence to support it as being anything else. If you will join with me in this crusade for life, we will become known as the true saviors of all humanity, and for all time. We will be the chosen ones who resurrected humanity out of the pit of total darkness bringing light and salvation to the Whole, to God, Brahma, Allah, the Source, Sea of Mind, the Creator, the Self. No matter what you call us, we are ONE. We are the thoughts of the Creator. Only by uniting together can we manifest this most magnificent dream! Always remember that I love you, the Cosmos loves you, and everyone who dreams of a better life, loves you. We all need to lovo you by loving each other, and more importantly, you must always **LOVE YOURSELF**!!!